THE CALPHALON® INTERNATIONAL COOKBOOK

by Anne Goodale Holmes

150 recipes featuring high nutrition, natural flavors, and professional cooking techniques to use in your own kitchen

THE CALPHALON INTERNATIONAL COOKBOOK —
What's In It for You?

The *CALPHALON INTERNATIONAL COOKBOOK* brings together the most important influences on the modern culinary scene — *your* scene! Here you'll find more than 150 recipe ideas from 18 different countries, recreated to capture modern notions about nutrition, flavor and freshness, calories and cholesterol, cooking ease and food costs — geared to a family kitchen, stocked with equipment once available only to professionals: your new *CALPHALON* cookware.

From France, Spain, Belgium, Italy, and many other countries we've adapted classic regional recipes to some of the recent French experiments in low-calorie cooking (*cuisine minceur*], but tempered by the growing demand here in the U.S. for fast, simple preparation. The *CALPHALON INTERNATIONAL COOKBOOK* tells how to plan menus and prepare traditional recipes by balancing, reducing, or eliminating cream, butter, egg yolks, fats, sugar and starches. We show how you can use your *CALPHALON* steamer to intensify natural flavor, freshness, and vitamins; how to use your flat pans (omelet, sauteuse, casserole, and saute pans) to caramelize natural sugars; how to substitute fresh herbs for salt and butter; where to reduce starches by the addition of fresh vegetables and new textures.

Above all, the *CALPHALON INTERNATIONAL COOKBOOK* is an idea book. Its basic techniques will guide beginners through some important discoveries about the magic chemistry of food, while experienced chefs may be inspired to delightful improvisations.

Among professionals — those who've been using *CALPHALON* cookware for years — there's a saying that "The more you know about cooking, the more you appreciate *CALPHALON*."

For my part, I hope that the more you know about cooking, the more you'll use your *CALPHALON INTERNATIONAL COOKBOOK*.

Good luck!
Good cooking!
Good eating!

— *ANNE GOODALE HOLMES*

Calphalon Cookware Index

TYPE OF RECIPE	RECOMMENDED PIECES	SIZE
For casseroles, baked meats or fish	CALPHALON casseroles	2–3–5 qt.
	CALPHALON deep casseroles	2½–5 qt.
	CALPHALON 2-handled sauciers	2½–5 qt.
For souffles	CALPHALON deep casseroles	2½–5 qt.
	CALPHALON 2-handled sauciers	2½–5 qt.
For Poule au pot, soup stocks, soups	CALPHALON stock pot	8–12 qt.
	CALPHALON sauce pan	8½ qt.
For omelets, sauteed vegetables Spanish tortilla	CALPHALON omelet pans	7–10–12 in. (depending on amounts in recipe)
For sauces	CALPHALON butter-warmer	2–cup
	CALPHALON shallow sauce pan	2½ qt.
	CALPHALON omelet pan	7–8 in.
For home-made yogurt	CALPHALON stock pot	8–12 qt.
	CALPHALON sauce pan	8½ qt.
For steaming rice, vegetables	CALPHALON steamer	4-qt. insert, 5-qt. bottom
For poaching fish, seafood	CALPHALON sauteuse	9½ in.
	CALPHALON saute pan	5 qt.
	CALPHALON omelet pan	12–14 in.
For baking chicken, ham, other meats	CALPHALON 2-handled sauteuse	5 qt.
	CALPHALON deep casserole	2½–5 qt.
	CALPHALON casserole	5–7½ qt.
For scallops, stuffed vegetables, range-top dishes to be passed under broiler	CALPHALON casserole LID	All sizes

TABLE OF CONTENTS

Menu-Planning

Americans visiting France for the first time express amazement that French people manage to stay so slender. How do they manage it, when the humblest lunch or dinner includes about five courses. The key fact is that such variety makes it possible—even vital—to keep portions small.

Variety is the Golden Rule in the New Cuisine. What's more, it requires no more effort than the heaping plate we grew up with, the old-fashioned, All-American, meat-and-potatoes meal.

An hors-d'oeuvre course can be as simple as a tray of radishes and butter, the soup no more than a clarified broth, dessert only a stewed fig in wine. But the total meal—its variety and emphasis on fresh, natural flavors—will result in a feeling of satisfaction far richer than the old "heaped plate."

To simplify your menu-planning, I've arranged this book in courses rather than chapters—which you can select from as if you were reading a menu or shopping in a farmer's market.

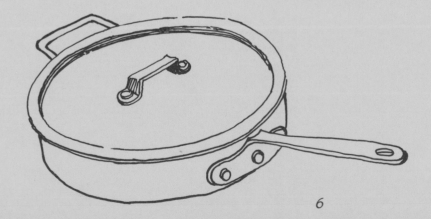

CHAPTER ONE

Hors d'Oeuvres, Canapes, and Snacks

HORS-d'OEUVRES, CANAPES, and SNACKS

In French, hors-d'oeuvres are foods prepared "outside the main effort." Still, we all know cooks who've made a fine reputation preparing hors-d'oeuvres as if they were the meal's high point. Complex or simple, hors-d'oeuvres hold an important place on your menu. They enlarge the stage, they give you more latitude in balancing a meal. If the cutlets are small, you can glorify your menu with an Easy Pate, Eggs Mayonnaise, Ham Coronets. If you're feeding a finicky family, or a motley gathering who may or may not be following some special regime, count on that marvelous hors-d'oeuvre course to help compensate for any gap that might occur later in the meal. And if your "main effort" is something absolutely terrific, here's another French expression to cheer you: l'appetit vient en mangeant. Nothing brings out an appetite like the first bite!

Pate en Gelée

Begin with *EASY BEEF PATE*, but instead of pressing mixture into a log, spread it into a gelatin mold prepared as follows:

Dissolve 3 beef bouillon cubes or 3 tablespoons bouillon crystals into 1 cup boiling water. Then lower heat, stir in bouillon plus one packet unflavored gelatin, and 2 tablespoons Maggi seasoning sauce. Stir till mixture clarifies. Then pour into pre-chilled 7-inch Calphalon omelet pan or gelatin mold, turning till mixture begins to take the shape of the pan. Chill till gelatin becomes firm, then fill mold with pate mixture and chill again. Keep refrigerated till serving time, then unmold and serve with small melba rounds.

Easy Beef Pate

The traditional ingredient for bestowing *shape* to a meat pate is tallow, lard, or some other animal fat. However, these ingredients do cut the flavor — to say nothing of their effect on the waistline. Here's a beautiful recipe for making beef pate from scratch — with little fat — and it can easily be adapted to leftover chicken, pork, veal, lamb, meatballs and meatloaf.

1 lb. ground beef
1 cup nonfat dried milk powder
1 cup each: celery, onions, carrots; washed, peeled,
*   and coursely chopped*
1/2 teaspoon salt
pinch white pepper
1 tablespoon Worchestershire sauce
3 tablespoons Maggi seasoning sauce
1/4 cup beef stock, reconstituted bouillon, or water

In your Calphalon omelet pan (12 inches), brown meat till uniformly cooked but not "sizzled." Spoon meat into Calphalon steamer or collander, then set steamer into warm omelet pan to drain. (If you cook with gas, leave pan over extinguished burner to stay warm. If you cook electrically, remove pan from heat.) While meat drains, simmer vegetables and seasonings in stock until tender. Then place all ingredients plus powdered milk in blender and blend mixture till smooth. (You may have to add more liquid, which should be warm.)

With a minimum of handling, shape blend into a log, wrap in waxed paper, and refrigerate at least 24 hours. Pate can then be served as is and sliced at the table. Or you can roll log just before serving in fresh grated parsley or toasted sesame seeds. For a classical touch, serve pate with crusty, oven-warmed bread, unsalted whipped butter, and a robust red wine — or cold apple cider garnished with a thin slice of lemon.

NOTE: If pate seems thin before shaping, soften 1 ounce (1 packet) unflavored gelatin in 1 teaspoon lemon juice, then dissolve in 1/2 cup hot beef bouillon. Blend this into pate and refrigerate 1/2 hour before shaping.

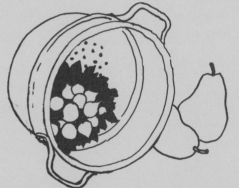

Pate en Croute

For picnics, parties, pot-lucks, and buffet-style serving, here's a simple recipe to transform *EASY BEEF PATE* into an elegant finger food.

Preheat oven to 425 degrees F.

1 — 1/4 cup enriched flour, sifted
1 teaspoon salt
1/4 cup peanut oil
1/4 cup milk

Mix flour and salt. Pour oil and milk into one measuring cup but don't stir. Then empty cup into flour mixture, stir till blended, and shape into ball. Between two sheets of waxed paper, roll dough into 1/8-inch thick oblong about 8 x 10 inches. Peel away top layer of waxed paper and wrap dough around *uncooled* pate log, tucking in both ends. Place log on ungreased cooky sheet, seam edge down, and bake on lowest oven rack about 20 minutes or till golden brown. Refrigerate till ready to serve, then slice thinly and place on a tray garnished with radish roses, water chestnuts, or wedges of green apple. Or let guests slice it at the table.

Coca Mallorquina

Americans who find their way to Spain's island paradise of Mallorca are usually dazzled by its cosmopolitan cuisine. But those who venture into the villages and byways never forget their first taste of Coca Mallorquina — a delectable vegetable tart sometimes identified as "spanish pizza." Among other distinctions, however, the Mallorcan coca intensifies in savor as it cools.

Preheat oven to 400 degrees F.

CRUST: Use recipe given for Pate en Croute, but roll dough into 11-inch circle to cover bottom and lower edge of Calphalon 3-quart sauteuse.

FILLING: *1 bunch fresh spinach*
             1 small spanish onion
             4 small salad tomatoes
             1 pinch salt
             1 pinch tarragon (dry is acceptable)

Wash spinach leaves, pat thoroughly dry, and arrange in a layer over dough. Scatter salt and tarragon, then arrange onion in rings, sliced as thinly as possible. End with layer of tomato slices, salt lightly. Bake coca on bottom oven rack for 30 minutes or till crust edges are golden brown. Cool thoroughly, then cut into wedges or small oblongs. Serve in salteuse or arrange on a platter.

Eggs Mayonnaise

Hard-boiled eggs, one for each person
1/8 cup mayonnaise (see chapter on sauces for
   making your own)
1/8 cup medium or sweet sherry
1 cup plain yogurt (see recipe)

Plunge cold eggs into boiling water, cook 12 minutes, then pass eggs under cold water for easy peeling. While eggs cool, mix mayonnaise, sherry, and yogurt. Then peel eggs, halve them lengthwise, and arrange cut side down on platter. Spoon mayonnaise sauce over each half till thoroughly coated, then sprinkle with fresh-grated parsley or drained capers. Chill till serving, then rearrange eggs if desired on bed of fresh Boston lettuce.

Ham Coronets

Thinly sliced boiled ham, unsmoked — plan on 2
  slices per person
1 small jar pimiento-stuffed Spanish olives
OR 1 can unsweetened pineapple wedges
OR 1 can unsweetened mandarin orange wedges

Place olive, pineapple, or orange near one corner of ham slice. Roll slice into cornucopia shape, arrange on a bed of lettuce, and sprinkle with grated parsley or slivered almonds.

Radishes au Buerre

Sweet, whipped, unsalted butter is the French equivalent of sour cream. *Radishes au Buerre* may be the simplest hors-d'oeuvre ever created — yet probably no other dish epitomizes the New Cuisine so well, with its complex interaction of textures and flavors.

RADISHES — 3 for each person
1/2 pint whipped, unsalted butter
1 loaf French or other hard-crusted bread

Wash and trim radishes, arrange them on a platter, and serve with bread, butter, cold white chablis or chilled rose wine.

Fresh Vegetables with Yogurt-Curry Sauce

Peel and slice an assortment of the following fresh vegetables:

zucchini
celery
cherry tomatoes
carrots
cauliflower tips
beetroots
broccoli stems
fresh mushroom caps

Mix 3 cups plain yogurt (see dessert chapter for making your own), 1 teaspoon seasoning salt, 1 tablespoon Maggi seasoning sauce, and 1/8 teaspoon powdered curry.

Arrange vegetables on a tray and serve accompanied by sauce.

Stuffed Mushrooms*

Wash and dry a number of large white mushrooms — about three per person. Remove stems and chop fine. Mix stems with the following:

1 cup dry grated bread crumbs
1/4 cup dry grated Parmesan cheese
1/4 cup fresh grated parsley
2 tablespoons Italian vermouth (optional)

In your Calphalon butter warmer, melt 1/8 cup salted butter and 1/8 cup peanut oil. Arrange mushroom caps in your Calphalon omelet pan (7 or 8 inch diameter) and fill each one with bread crumb mixture. Pour heated butter-and-oil blend over each mushroom. Slip pan under broiler for about 10 minutes or until filling begins to brown. Serve as soon as possible.

* Also see recipe for MUSHROOMS MILANO

Cheese Canapes

Until you make these exquisite, bite-size popovers yourself — and the following recipe for *BEACH BALLS* — you'll never believe such simple ingredients can produce such splendor!

> *1 cup boiling water*
> *1/2 cup salted butter (1/4 lb. stick)*
> *1/2 cup enriched, all-purpose flour*
> *1/2 cup grated parmesan cheese*
> *1 pinch each: powdered onion*
> *cayenne pepper*
> *salt*
> *2 eggs*

Boil water in Calphalon butter warmer, add butter, stir in seasonings and flour. Stir over low heat till smooth. Then remove from heat and stir in eggs one at a time. Drop mixture by teaspoonfuls onto ungreased cooky sheet, then bake 30 minutes at 350° F. Recipe makes 4 dozen (at least!) bite-size delicacies to serve with aperitifs or as an hors d'oeuvre course with a tray of raw vegetables.

Beach Balls

1/2 lb. fresh, shelled clams, chopped fine
OR small (7½ or 8-ounce) can minced clams
1/2 cup butter
1/2 teaspoon poultry seasoning
1/4 teaspoon salt
1 cup flour
4 eggs

Drain clams. Save liquor and add enough water to equal 1 cup. Follow recipe for making *CHEESE CANAPES*. Spoon batter by teaspoons onto greased cooky sheet and bake 10 minutes in oven preheated to 350° F. Makes about 60 delectable canapes which should be kept refrigerated till serving and then reheated quickly in a medium oven on an aluminum baking sheet.

Sauces,
Dips
and
a Word
about
Herbs

C. SCHNEIDER

CHAPTER TWO

SAUCES, DIPS, and A WORD ABOUT HERBS

In the world almanac of gastronomy, nearly every nation rates a page based at least on one of its sauces or seasonings. France has its mayonnaise, bechamel, and its version of the Dutch hollandiase. Spain has its all-i-oli (garlic sauce), Polynesia its sweet-and-sour marinades, and once in Paris I was even offered a sauce americane — ketchup!

Many of these exquisite seasonings might bring on an attack of gout if devoured too lavishly — but the New Cuisine is a celebration of natural perfection through moderation. The following recipes for sauces, dips, and seasonings invite you and your guests to sample the ecstasy of restraint. If a tablespoon of sauce per serving is good, a teaspoon might be better. And in the use of herbs, your own judgment may be best of all.

Very few cooks would have trouble distinguishing between a bouquet of dried flowers and a newly picked nosegay. The difference between dried and fresh herbs is probably even greater. You can't make a chervil soup or prepare parsleyed potatoes without absolutely fresh herbs, chopped and added at the very last minute. On the other hand, some seasonings are so strong that drying brings them under control: saffron, sage, rosemary, bayleaf, pepper, paprika, some say even garlic and onion, fall into this category.

In many cases, you'll just have to taste as you go, in order to decide whether a fresh herb will serve you better than a dried one, or a dried one better than none at all.

Mayonnaise

No bottle or jar will ever quite produce the equal of the mayonnaise made in your own kitchen. The following recipe is a classic mayonnaise especially recommended for cold lobster, shrimp, salmon, or artichokes.

2 eggs
2 cups peanut or very fresh olive oil
2 tablespoons white or red wine vinegar
Pinch white pepper
Pinch salt

Break eggs carefully, separate yolks, and drop them into a small-bottom bowl. Beat yolks till you're sure they won't get any lighter or foamier. Measure oil into beaker or pitcher which will pour with a very fine stream. The trick of making mayonnaise is to add the oil in a very fine stream in the beginning, continuing to beat the yolks at high speed as you pour. When the mayonnaise begins to separate into heavy curds, mix in the vinegar and seasonings to taste.

If mayonnaise never quite thickens, it's probably because the oil was added too fast in the beginning. You can always rescue a failed mayonnaise by starting over with fresh egg yolks in an immaculate bowl and adding the original mixture at the end.

Easy Bearnaise

Chop fresh tarragon leaves finely, to equal 1/2 teaspoonful, or powder 1 teaspoon dried tarragon between your thumb and index finger, and add it to one cup of mayonnaise. Chill for at least an hour, and longer if possible.

New Cuisine White Sauce

In your Calphalon butter-warmer or the top of a small double boiler, mix the following:

> 3 cups nonfat powdered milk
> 1/2 cup corn starch
> 1 teaspoon salt

When dry ingredients are thoroughly combined, add:

> 2 cups water
> 1/4 cups peanut oil

Cook over boiling water or low heat, stirring constantly till the first bubble appears. If sauce is too thick, add water, and salt to taste. Sauce may be reheated just before serving, but will become thin after too much cooking.

Garden Sauce

A piquant marinade, ideal for fresh or lightly steamed vegetables, or broiled steak.

> 2 cups sliced radishes
> 1/2 cup sliced scallions
> 1/2 cup white wine vinegar
> 1/8 cup water
> 2 teaspoons soy sauce
> 2 teaspoons brown sugar

Stir all ingredients together, chill at least one hour, and serve in a sauce dish at the table.

Cheese Sauce

Superb over little thin pancakes stuffed with cooked spinach or ham, and an ideal topping for baked leftover vegetables.

To *NEW CUISINE WHITE SAUCE*, add 1 cup grated parmesan cheese and stir over low heat till blended.

OR — substitute 1 cup grated gruyere cheese to *WHITE SAUCE* recipe, omitting oil.

Polynesian Sauce

Delicious when spooned sparingly over broiled ham slices, pork chops — or hamburgers!

Juice drained from small tin of pineapple slices or tidbits
1/8 cup brown sugar
1/4 teaspoon mustard powder
1/8 cup Maggi seasoning sauce
1/8 cup red wine vinegar
2 tablespoons cornstarch

Cook and stir over low heat in your Calphalon butter warmer till first bubble appears. Remove from heat and stir in pineapple chunks. Serve at once over meat or offer sauce separately at the table.

Boiled Dressing Dorothea

An old-fashioned recipe, *Boiled Dressing Dorothea* may be Dixie's finest contribution to the New Cuisine — and especially to cole slaw!

1 — 1/4 cup water
3 tablespoons lemon juice
1 tablespoon white granulated sugar
1 teaspoon salt
3 tablespoons corn starch
1 pinch celery seed
1/2 teaspoon Dijon mustard
1 dash Tabasco sauce
1 dash angostura bitters

Stir these ingredients in Calphalon butter warmer over low heat till thick. Remove from heat and beat in two egg yolks. Replace mixture over heat, and slowly add 3 to 4 tablespoons condensed milk, stirring till mixture comes just to the boil. Remove from heat, correct for seasonings, and stir over cold water to prevent dressing from getting a skin. May be kept for several days in refrigerator.

Easy Hollandaise

Follow recipe for *NEW CUISINE WHITE SAUCE*. When mixture begins to boil, remove from heat and stir in the juice from 2 fresh lemons. Add more salt if necessary.

Blue Cheese Salad Dressing

1/2 cup crumbled blue cheese
1/2 cup plain yogurt
1/4 teaspoon Tabasco sauce
2 cups mayonnaise (see recipe)
1/2 teaspoon salt

Mix all ingredients thoroughly and chill at least an hour before serving. A small amount of dressing can be kept in the refrigerator as a "culture" which will thicken and can be reused several times by adding only mayonnaise and salt.

Mint-Vinegar Sauce

This recipe was given to me by a man who thought he hated lamb because it was always served to him with a little "pot of green toothpaste" — mint jelly. The following recipe changed his mind, and if you know someone who can't abide lamb, don't be surprised if you work the same miracle! The secret is absolutely fresh mint, chopped fine and added just before serving.

1/4 cup white vinegar
2 tablespoons white granulated sugar
1 cup water
1/4 cup finely chopped fresh mint leaves

Stir ingredients together and serve in a sauce dish at the table as an accompaniment to lamb chops, cutlets, or *ROAST LAMB MUSCADET* (see chapter on meats for recipe).

Sensational Tartar Sauce

Follow the recipe for home-made mayonnaise. To each cup of mayonnaise, add 1/2 cup plain yogurt*; 2 teaspoons medium sherry, and 1/2 cup fresh grated parsley. Salt if desired.

* See recipe for making your own yogurt in the chapter on *DESSERTS*.

All-i-Oli
(Spanish Garlic Sauce)

Traditionally served with nothing more than hearty peasant bread, *All-i-Oli* is also pure ambrosia when served as a mere kiss on broiled tomatoes or steak.

Follow recipe for classic *MAYONNAISE*. Add 1/2 teaspoon fresh lemon juice, powdered garlic to desired intensity, and salt as needed.

Soups

CHAPTER THREE

SOUPS

If you own a blender, you know you can make a hearty and delicious soup out of almost anything. Yesterday's casserole? Put it in the blender with a little milk or bouillon. Leftover spaghetti, vegetables, even pancakes form a good base to which you can add your own chopped fresh herbs and seasonings to give your soup "personality."

Here are a few tips for perking up a "Cream of Leftover Soup" — which has only one drawback. When friends ask for the recipe, they'll think you're joking when you answer that there is none!

- Always bone chicken or fish very carefully before blending.
- Use liquids drained from cooked vegetables as part of the liquid in your soup. Don't try to save these liquids for more than three or four days, however.
- A teaspoon of lemon juice will help reduce an over-salty flavor.
- A too-thin soup can be heartened by gradually stirring dehydrated potato flakes into the mixture till you get desired consistency.
- If your soup base contains cheese, do not heat soup to boiling point, or cheese will curdle.
- For last-minute seasoning, stir in Maggi Seasoning Sauce to taste, or top with one of the following: 1/2 cup chopped chives, parsley, scallions, grated parmesan cheese, or 1/2 teaspoon paprika.

Watercress Soup

This delectable soup can be served piping hot in winter, or cold, like its distant cousin *Vichyssoise*.

> 6 medium-size red potatoes
> 1 medium-size onion
> 6 cups white stock
> OR 6 cups reconstituted bouillon crystals
> 1 egg yolk
> 1/2 cup cream or concentrated milk
> salt and pepper to taste
> 1 bunch fresh watercress

Wash and peel potatoes, remove eyes carefully, and cut into small pieces. Cut up onion, and place potatoes, onion, salt, pepper, butter and stock to simmer in large Calphalon sauteuse. When potatoes and onions are tender, mash, sieve or blend them into a smooth puree. Beat egg yolk, stir it into cream, and warm mixture by adding a cup of hot soup gradually. Then pour mixture into soup, stirring at low heat to prevent curdling. Just before serving, stir in finely cut watercress leaves (no stems) and add butter.

Cream Nivernaise
(Cream of Carrot Soup)

Some call Nevers the carrot capital of France — a region where cooks have devoted many generations to enhancing the savor of this humble vegetable. When you've tasted *Creme Nivernaise*, I think you'll agree they've done a remarkable job.

10 small, tender carrots
2 tablespoons butter
2 tablespoons flour
3 cups white stock: veal or chicken broth, or
    reconstituted chicken bouillon crystals
3 cups extra rich milk
3 stalks parsley
2 chopped shallots
OR 2 thin slices of onion
1 each: salt
        pepper
        nutmeg
1 egg yolk
1/4 cup cream

Peel carrots, cut into small pieces, and simmer about 10 minutes with butter in your 9-inch Calphalon sauteuse. Stir to prevent browning. Remove from heat. Pour milk, flour, and seasonings into blender, then add carrots and blend till mixture is as smooth as possible. Pour mixture back into salteuse, add stock, and simmer covered for about 40 minutes stirring occasionally. Add well-beaten egg yolk to cream, then slowly pour about a half-cup of hot soup into mixture to prevent curdling. Add this mixture to soup, stirring constantly, to "bind" soup. Serve as soon as possible.

Chervil Soup

A staple in France and England, chervil soup is almost unknown in the U.S. This is undoubtedly due to the fact that fresh chervil is a rarity in the States except in dried form, which is totally lacking in personality. But if you know someone who grows it, this friendship is worth encouraging! Or — you can buy a pot of chervil at most nurseries to flourish on your kitchen window sill.

Follow directions for WATERCRESS SOUP, substituting sweet, fresh-chopped chervil in place of the cress.

Green Gazpacho
(Catalonian Summer Soup)

For most Americans Spanish cooking is an undiscovered pleasure — known only through its famous *paellas* and Andalusian *gazpacho*, made with tomatoes and served cold. Basically gazpacho is a peasant dish which varies from region to region throughout coastal Iberia, depending on which ingredients are locally grown, cheap and plentiful. I think you'll agree that *Green Gazpacho* deserves to be better known.

> 1 large onion
> 1 fresh bell pepper
> 1 medium cucumber
> 1/2 cup parsley leaves
> 3 sprigs fresh mint
> 2 tablespoons peanut oil or very fresh olive oil
> 1 tablespoon white wine vinegar
> 1 pinch each: salt and pepper
> 5 cups water

Coarse-chop vegetables, removing seeds from bell pepper, and place all ingredients but water in blender. Blend till mixture is puréed. Put water into serving tureen, add puree, and refrigerate for as long as possible to intensify flavors before serving. Serve cold, garnished with green olive slices or pine nuts.

Sopa de Res
(Nicaraguan Beef Soup)

Born of humble and fairly ordinary ingredients, this hearty soup boasts a flavor that intrigues and delights almost everyone who samples it.

2 lbs. beef neckbones with meat (or more if you wish)
3-4 quarts water
1 chopped onion
1 clove garlic crushed
OR garlic powder to taste
1 bell pepper, seeded and chopped
2 chopped tomatoes
1 cup cooked carrots with liquid
2 sliced, cooked baking bananas
1 cup yuca (or substitute cooked artichoke hearts)
2 ears steamed corn cut into 1-inch pieces

Simmer beef bones, water, onion and garlic till meat is cooked. Remove meat from bones and return to *strained* broth. Then add green pepper, tomatoes, and pre-cooked or steamed vegetables. Reheat soup. Just before serving, stir in 3 tablespoons chopped celantro or Chinese parsley, 2 tablespoons lemon juice, salt and pepper to taste.

Mediterranean Soupe de Poisson

From Spain's Balearic Isles to the toe of Italy's boot, this soup is a staple in the Mediterranean Basin. Its ingredients vary enormously, depending on the day's catch or yesterday's leftovers. The traditional seasoning is garlic, as in many hot countries, but many epicures find it just as enjoyable when the garlic is only a whisper instead of a shout.

> *2 lbs. assorted fish — bass, perch, cod, salmon,*
> *1 bay leaf*
> *2 tablespoons oil*
> *1 slice each: onion and lemon*
> *1 sprig parsley*
> *1 branch of celery with leaves*
> *2 cups white wine*
> *4 medium tomatoes, peeled and cut up*
> *To taste: salt, pepper, and garlic.*

In 9-inch Calphalon sauteuse, bring all ingredients except fish to a boil, turn down heat and simmer 15 minutes, covered. Then add fish and poach for 15 minutes more. Remove and drain fish; skin and bone it carefully, and place fish in blender. Remove bay leaf and onion slice from broth, and pour remainder into blender. (You may have to blend only half of fish and broth at a time.) Blend till soup is smooth, and serve hot. If soup tends to separate, use any of the following "binders":

- *Two egg yolks, beaten smooth and mixed with a cup of soup before adding* — OR
- *1 cup dehydrated potato flakes* — OR
- *1 cup nonfat dry milk powder* — OR
- *Serve Mallorcan style, by adding a slice of brown bread for each person, and simmering an extra 10 minutes after blending.*

NOTE: If you're making *Soupe de Poisson* to use up leftover fish, it's easier to bone and skin fish before placing it in broth to simmer. You should also reduce simmering time to about 7 minutes.

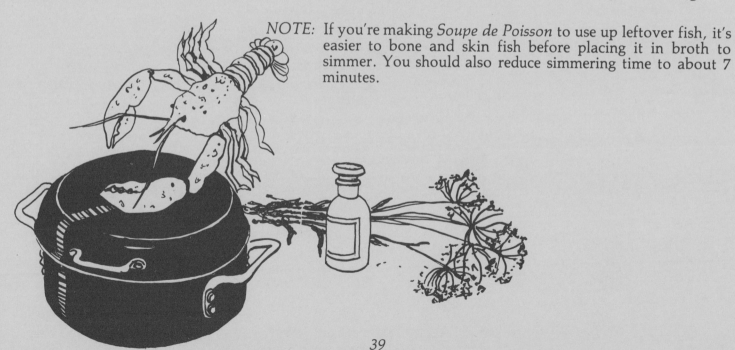

Almond Soup

We owe a vote of thanks to Southern Spain for this milky white concoction — if only for destroying the notion that it's a long leap "from soup to nuts". Traditionally served cold with a rose petal floating on top, Almond Soup is a work of art as well as a culinary masterpiece.

1 lb. blanched almonds
2 tablespoons peanut oil or very fresh olive oil
2 teaspoons white wine vinegar
1½ cups seeded white grapes
4 cups ice water
1 clove garlic
OR powdered garlic to taste
salt to taste

Place almonds, oil, salt, water and garlic in blender and puree till smooth. Refrigerate soup to intensify flavor. (Store in blender if you wish.) Just before serving, stir in vinegar and peeled grapes. Pour soup into chilled glass bowls or sherbet dishes, and garnish each one with a rose petal.

Chilled Avocado Soup

Here's another summer soup to pique dull appetites. Warm weather usually increases a luncheon or dinner guest's tolerance for spices — but if you like, you may substitute 2 tablespoons Maggi Seasoning Sauce for chili powder.

> *Follow recipe for potato soup base given under*
>   *WATERCRESS SOUP*
> *(OR — Blend one can cooked new potatoes with*
>   *3 cups extra-rich milk*
>   *1 tablespoon powdered onion*
>   *1 tablespoon chicken bouillon crystals*
>   *and salt to taste)*
> *1 large or 2 small ripe avocados*
> *1/4 teaspoon chili powder*

The variant for making potato soup isn't quite as good, but on hot days, the cook as well as the table guests deserves special consideration. If you use a blender, you may have to blend potato base in two installments. From there on, the procedure is the same.

Peel, stone, and mash avocado, mix in chili powder, and add this mixture to base. Pour soup into serving tureen, and refrigerate for as long as possible before serving.

Chinese Egg-Drop Soup

At first glance, egg-drop soup is a thin broth that promises to whet rather than slake an appetite. But unlike other Oriental dishes, its effect takes over slowly. To keep broth clear, the egg must be added with care, so that it bursts into clear, free-form "flowers" instead of a murky paste.

4 cups strained White Stock
OR — 4 cups water and 4 tablespoons chicken
  bouillon crystals
1 handful frozen tiny peas or small fresh
  garden peas
2 eggs
Salt if necessary

Heat stock or bouillon to just below boiling. Add peas, and while they simmer, stir eggs in glass measuring beaker with fork till thoroughly mixed but not foamy. Then — in as fine a stream as possible — pour eggs into simmering broth without stirring. If you use a wide-based salteuse, pour in circles to introduce egg all through broth. Top with finely chopped *fresh* parsley if desired and serve at once.

Cold Cucumber Soup

As you may have noticed, cold soups form a major part of the New Cuisine — and perhaps the "New" part, since most Americans are accustomed to piping hot soups on winter nights. Yet many soups offered cold by tradition taste just as good hot: it's only that added cooking breaks down the texture and sometimes — but not always — changes the original flavor. Cucumber soup may be served hot if you wish; and unless you tell, most people will be surprised at its provenance.

> *4 large cucumbers, peeled and sliced*
> *1 tablespoon grated onion*
> *1/4 cup butter*
> *1 pinch salt*
> *1/4 teaspoon curry powder*
> *2 cups white stock or reconstituted chicken bouillon crystals*
> *1 dash cayenne pepper*
> *1 teaspoon fresh lemon juice*
> *1½ cups cream or condensed milk*
> *1/2 cup freshly chopped chives*

Place cucumber, onion, and butter in Calphalon sauteuse and saute till transparent. Add salt, curry, cayenne, and stock, heat till boiling and simmer 10 minutes. Then pour mixture into blender, and puree. Stir in lemon juice and cream. Serve with chopped chives as topping.

Pumpkin Soup

Here's another hot-or-cold soup, with an off-beat taste that pleases as well as baffles most Americans. This recipe comes from the Canary Islands, but variants abound in hot climates where pumpkins or calabashes make up a year-round staple.

2 pounds cooked pumpkin
2 tablespoons peanut or very fresh olive oil
1 onion
1 small sweet red pepper
1 clove garlic or 1 teaspoon powdered garlic
2 tablespoons finely chopped parsley
2 medium ripe tomatoes

2 teaspoons paprika
1/2 teaspoon cumin powder
1/2 teaspoon brown sugar
1 pinch saffron
2 teaspoons white wine vinegar
Salt and pepper to taste

If pumpkin is fresh, simmer in Calphalon sauteuse with a quart of water till tender. Or — blend canned pumpkin into same amount of water and simmer over low heat. In calphalon butter warmer, saute finely chopped onion, sweet pepper, and garlic in oil. When about half cooked, add peeled tomatoes, parsley, paprika, cumin, and saffron. Cook about three more minutes, then add to pumpkin. Season soup with sugar, salt, pepper, and vinegar, then simmer for another half-hour. Mash, sieve, or put soup through blender to produce a fine puree (you may want to add water or milk), and serve either hot or chilled for at least four hours.

Dixie Crab-and-Corn Chautauqua

Another recipe rescued from a Southern pantry, this unusual soup makes a celebration of rather mild ingredients.

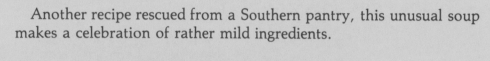

1/2 pound crab meat, cooked
1/2 cup chopped chives
2 cups steamed or canned corn
2 cups NEW CUISINE WHITE SAUCE (see recipe)
salt and pepper to taste
1 cup concentrated or condensed milk

Make white sauce according to recipe. Add flakes of crabmeat, chives, corn, salt, pepper, and milk. Soup should be thick but you may wish to thin slightly with milk or white wine. Serve hot with oven-warmed French bread or corn muffins.

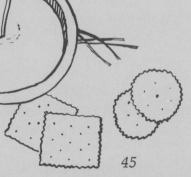

Mongole Puree
(Tomato and Pea Soup)

I have never been sure why the French named this highly refined soup in honor of the Mongols. It may result from the fact that the toughest of vegetables can be used — the last of the summer crop — yet their deep, rich flavor survives the onslaught of the sieve.

> *1 pound large garden peas, shelled*
> *OR — one 10-ounce package frozen peas*
> *1 hambone or cube of salt pork*
> *1 medium onion, cut up*
> *1 large celery stalk with leaves, cut up*
> *2 medium or 1 large carrot, peeled and sliced*
> *1 clove*
> *1 bay leaf*
> *1/4 teaspoon thyme*
> *3 medium or two large tomatoes*
> *3 quarts water*

Simmer all ingredients together for 4 hours. Remove bone, bay leaf, and clove. Remove as much fat as possible from broth, and strain. Put remaining vegetables through sieve, straining out skins and seeds. Serve soup hot with cheese croutons.

Eggs

CHAPTER FOUR

EGGS

Eggs have been called one of nature's most perfect foods — immaculately packaged at the point of delivery. The poorest peasant can labor on a diet of eggs instead of meat, while the most effete of aristocrats demands his egg course with every meal. "Boiling eggs" is probably the first cooking lesson you ever had — and by now you probably know at least a dozen good ways to serve an egg.

Therefore, I've chosen the following recipes for their very special qualities.

Huevos al Nido
(Eggs in a Nest)

Variously known as "Hobo Eggs" and "Red-eye Eggs," this recipe depends mainly on a watchful eye from the cook. Its success usually derives from knowing in advance whether those who will eat them like their eggs cooked hard or soft.

FOR EACH SERVING USE:
>*1 thin slice very fresh bread*
>*1 egg*
>*1 strip of bacon*
>*(Grated parsley — OPTIONAL)*

Saute bacon over low heat in Calphalon omelet pan, draining and saving fat till bacon reaches golden "crumbly stage. Remove crusts from bread, then grease muffin tins or custard cups with bacon fat, and gently form bread slices into "nests," one slice per cup. Break an egg into each nest and sprinkle with crumbled bacon. Bake in moderate oven (350° F.) till points of nest are golden brown — or till egg is white in appearance. Top with grated parsley and serve for breakfast, lunch, or dinner.

Repuffing Souffle
— with Cheese, Seafood, or Vegetables

The aim of this book is to simplify as far as possible the last-minute procedures that make up a large part of the New Cuisine. One of the nicest things about this recipe is that you really can make it ahead of time and reheat it just before serving. Miraculously — it *will* rise again!

> 3 tablespoons butter
> 2 tablespoons cornstarch
> 1/2 teaspoon salt
> 1 dash white pepper
> 1 cup condensed or concentrated milk
> 1 cup grated swiss or gruyere cheese
> OR — 1 cup crabmeat (steamed and drained first)
> OR — 1 cup washed and finely chopped vegetables
> 4 eggs

Melt butter in Calphalon butter-warmer, blend in cornstarch, salt, and pepper. Remove from heat and stir in milk, then cook and stir till mixture is thickened. Grease 8-inch (2-quart) Calphalon sauteuse and line bottom with cheese, crabmeat, or chopped vegetables and spoon mixture over all. Separate eggs. Beat yolks till frothy and stir thin into casserole. Using a clean bowl, beat whites till stiff and fold them into souffle. Place sauteuse in a pan of hot water and bake in oven preheated to 350° F. for 1¼ hours. Serves four generously — or more if souffle precedes several courses.

TO REPUFF — Leave souffle in sauteuse. Reheat as you baked it, in a pan of hot water in 350-degree oven for 20 to 30 minutes.

Baked Eggs Asparagus

This delicious recipe boasts many variants, but the one that follows combines not only classic flavors but a contrast in textures. When asparagus is out of season, you can substitute canned asparagus tips, but they must be of the finest quality.

2 cups NEW CUISINE WHITE SAUCE (see recipe)
1 bunch tender asparagus tips
6 eggs (or one per serving)
1 small can water chestnuts
1 cup grated Swiss or gruyere cheese
2 tablespoons Maggi seasoning sauce
1 dash each: salt, pepper, curry powder

Steam asparagus lightly in your Calphalon steamer. Drain and mix liquid into white sauce. Blend seasonings into sauce. Grease 8- or 9-inch Calphalon sauteuse and spread half of sauce on the bottom. Drain water chestnuts, quarter them, and spread equally over layer of sauce. Break eggs carefully into sauce, keeping yolks intact and spacing them evenly around sauteuse. Cover eggs with remaining sauce, top with grated cheese, and bake no more than 20 minutes in medium 350° F.) oven. Serve in sauteuse, within a half-hour or so.

Quiche Alsace

Many French recipes use bacon as a flavoring, rather than as a main ingredient, and that's why I prefer this recipe for quiche.

1 unbaked pie-crust (Use any recipe, or follow
recipe in COCA MALLORQUINA)
1/2 slice bacon per person to be served
1½ cups aged swiss or gruyere cheese
(that is, medium sharp)
3 eggs
1½ cups condensed milk
1½ teaspoons salt
1 dash each: white pepper, nutmeg, cayenne

Preheat oven to 375° F. Fry bacon slowly till golden brown, draining as it cooks. Make crust and use it to line decorative pie plate or Calphalon 8-inch omelet pan. Crumble bacon fine over bottom of crust. Sprinkle cheese over bacon. In medium bowl, beat eggs, milk, and seasonings till well combined. Place crust on middle oven rack and pour in liquid ingredients. Bake 35 to 40 minutes till knife comes out clean. Cool 10 minutes, then serve. *QUICHE* can be baked ahead and reheated, or served cold.

Omelette Piperade
(Basque Omelet)

Like the Basque country itself, a Basque omelet is something between French scrambled eggs and a Spanish omelet: more interesting than the former, more delicate than the latter.

FOR EACH TWO PERSONS, USE:
> 2 tablespoons peanut or very fresh olive oil
> 1 small bell pepper
> 1 small onion
> 1 small garlic clove
> OR — 1/4 teaspoon garlic powder
> 1 ripe beefsteak tomato
> 2 tablespoons chopped ham
> 1 tablespoon butter
> 4 eggs
> Salt and pepper to taste

Seed green pepper. Peel, seed and chop tomato. Chop and mash garlic clove. Slice pepper and onion thinly and saute in oil with garlic and tomato, using seven-inch Calphalon omelet pan. Add ham and simmer mixture for 20 to 30 minutes, till tender. Stir in butter. When melted, add eggs lightly beaten. If necessary add salt and pepper, stirring as little as possible so that eggs will set without overcooking. Serve at once, from the pan.

Tortilla Espanola
(Spanish Omelet)

The Spanish omelet owes nothing at all to the Mexican tortilla — with which it's often confused — nor is it anything like the Basque omelet. In Spain a *tortilla* is an omelet customarily made with potatoes and cooked into a solid cake that can be served cold at a picnic as well as hot at the dinner table. The characteristic flavor is olive oil — but unless you have a source for getting this very fresh, I suggest peanut oil instead.

> *4 eggs*
> *2 large red potatoes*
> *2 large onions*
> *1/2 cup olive oil or peanut oil*
> *salt to taste*

Peel potatoes, removing eyes carefully, and dice them with onions in quarter-inch cubes. Pour oil into 9-inch Calphalon omelet pan, heat and stir in salted vegetables. Cover and simmer till tender, stirring occasionally. Meantime, beat eggs well. With slotted spoon, remove vegetables from pan and stir into eggs. Pour all back into pan and cook at low heat till omelet comes away from the sides. Then slide onto a plate and turn omelet back into the pan. Omelet is done when fork comes out clean. Serve plain or sprinkled with finely grated fresh parsley.

Chicken

CHAPTER FIVE

CHICKEN

Chicken is probably one of the most interesting, versatile, and economical staples of the New Cuisine. Most the the chickens on the market today are labeled "fryers" — but this is a matter of weight, not quality. Fryers can also be stuffed and roasted, broiled, simmered, and stewed.

Whole chickens are cheaper than dismembered ones and often on sale when others are not. If you buy a few for the freezer and decide later you want them cut up, here are some easy directions:

USE A SHARP, SERRATED FREEZER KNIFE. Thaw chicken thoroughly, remove neck and giblets from cavity. Suspend chicken by one leg and cut through skin at hip joint, guiding knife between thighbone and socket. When the joint is exposed, you can see tendon that holds bones together. Saw at it gently till body separates from leg. Separate thighs from legbones and wings from body in the same manner.

To divide breast from back, hold carcass up to light so you can see where ribs on far side come together in a herringbone pattern. Saw downward on far side through these inverted V's as far as you can. Then turn carcass and cut through the other side. Spread back and breast as wide as possible, and continue sawing till two halves of carcass separate.

Divide back into two parts as follows. Bend chicken back double as far as possible and slip knife into fold to find natural separation, where it will divide most easily. To divide breast into two parts, saw downward through V-shaped breastbone. This is the hardest part of the cutting, since you'll have to saw through center of breastbone. (Or — a kitchen cleaver will do it on one chop!) If you meet too much resistance, spread the breast apart as you work. This will crack the bone neatly along the centerline. Then cut meat slowly, taking care not to let skin separate from flesh.

The second chicken will be easier to cut up than the first, and by the fourth or fifth time you'll feel like a pro — and also have saved enough money to get another chicken free!

Chinese Chicken

This is the easiest yet most original chicken recipe I've ever encountered. Technique, however, is everything. Follow directions to the letter and you'll come out with chicken delicately flavored, firm-fleshed, and encased under a crisp, golden skin puffed up like chicken Kiev.

1 chicken for each 4 persons
salt and pepper to taste
1/4 cup fresh lemon juice
3/4 cup water (approximately)

Salt and pepper each chicken piece (quarters or smaller), then brush with lemon juice to keep flesh white and firm. Place pieces rib-side down in 12-inch Calphalon sauteuse or baking pan, and broil quickly till brown, about 5 minutes. Turn pieces skin side up, cover bottom of pan with water and return chicken to hot oven (450° F.) and bake 20 to 25 minutes or till skin is brown and puffed. Serve in Calphalon pan or remove to platter.

Coq aux Corinthes
(Chicken with White Raisins)

My thanks go to a Belgian chef for this elegant recipe, which exalts a humble bird to regal status.

1 cup white raisins
1 cup chablis wine
1 large frying chicken, cut up
1/2 cup flour

1/2 teaspoon salt
1 pinch white pepper
1/2 cup condensed or concentrated milk

Soak raisins in wine overnight or at least 4 hours before serving. Simmer neck and giblets in Calphalon butter warmer, using about a cup of lightly salted water. Remove all fat from chicken pieces; mix salt, pepper, and flour and dust this mixture over chicken. Brown chicken in your largest Calphalon sauteuse (3- or 5-quart), lightly oiled. Remove pieces when golden on both sides. Drain raisins, reserving liquor, and set aside. Pour liquor into sauteuse with remnants of floured chicken and bring to high boil stirring constantly to burn off alcohol and slightly thicken liquor. Arrange chicken in sauteuse and pour broth from neck and giblets over all. Bake in medium oven (about 350° F.) basting occasionally and sprinkling raisins over chicken during last half-hour of baking. Remove from oven and draw sauce from bottom of sauteuse with baster, placing it in a pre-heated bowl. Skim off any fat. Stir in condensed milk, pour over chicken and serve at once, either in sauteuse or deep serving dish.

Chicken Nicole

The rich golden glaze on this chicken requires careful treatment of the sherry. It must be caramelized a little bit at a time to brown it and remove the alcohol.

1 frying chicken, cut up
2 tablespoons butter (or more if necessary)
salt
Maggi Seasoning Sauce
1/2 cup medium sherry

Salt chicken lightly and sprinkle each piece with a few drops Maggi Seasoning Sauce. Brown chicken in butter in large Calphalon omelet pan or sauteuse, turning frequently. Use low heat. When chicken is golden on both sides, remove from pan allowing as much fat as possible to drip back into pan. Turn heat high and when butter begins to sizzle, add a dash of sherry. Sherry will steam, then boil, and gradually reduce to syrup. At that point, add a little more sherry and continue till you've carmelized the full amount. Turn down heat and arrange chicken in pan again, basting it with sauce. Continue cooking chicken partly covered and basting frequently till tender, about 20 minutes. Serve at once.

Poule au Pot
(Savory Stewed Chicken)

Once upon a time this recipe worked like magic to turn a tough old hen into a tender beauty. For modern cooks, it boasts an added charm: You can start with a whole chicken, straight from the freezer. If you prefer to serve it in pieces, the separation happens almost by itself after cooking.

1 chicken
1 cup each: chopped onion, celery, carrots
1 bayleaf
1 pinch thyme
1 teaspoons salt
8 new potatoes
OR — 1 cup NEW CUISINE WHITE SAUCE

Place chicken in Calphalon sauce pan or bottom of Calphalon steamer. (Must be deep enough to cook chicken with cover on.) Add salt, seasonings, and vegetables, plus enough water to fill bottom of pot to depth of two inches. Simmer slowly till chicken breast is tender (test with skewer rather than fork to minimize number of holes in skin). Cooking will take at least two hours for frozen bird, only one hour for a thawed one. During last 20 minutes add peeled new potatoes to pot and cook till tender.

At this point you can choose from several different ways of serving. One way is to place whole chicken on the center of a serving platter, heaped with vegetables used in cooking and surrounded by parsleyed new potatoes. The broth can be skimmed and served separately or thicken with *NEW CUISINE WHITE SAUCE.* Another method is to divide chicken in pieces, arrange on ovenproof serving platter, and brown them quickly under the broiler — no more than 5 minutes. Or you can disjoint chicken and serve it with vegetables in a deep casserole under thickened sauce, garnishing the whole dish with freshly chopped parsley.

Chicken Benne
(Roast Chicken with Sesame Seeds)

"Benne" is an African dialect word for sesame seeds. For those who like a contrast in textures, the crisp exterior and tender flesh of Chicken Benne are the ultimate.

> 1 large or 2 small fryers, cut up
> 3 tablespoons lemon juice
> 1/2 tablespoon salt
> 1 dash Angostura bitters on each piece
> 1/2 cup sesame seeds

Brush undersides of chicken with lemon juice and arrange on baking sheet. Brush top sides with remaining lemon juice and bitters. Salt lightly and sprinkle with sesame seeds. Roast at 350° F. for 40 minutes or so, depending on size of pieces. (Smaller pieces cook faster.) Test for doneness by inserting small knife into underside of breast near bone. If juice flows out clear instead of pink, chicken is done and ready to serve.

Chalupas
(Chicken-Stuffed Mexican Pancakes)

This recipe is the gift of a Mexican friend who thought I could use an education in the subtler forms of Latin-American cooking. She was absolutely right, and deserves my heartfelt thanks. Celia's *CHALUPAS* are still one of the most interesting chicken dishes I've ever had.

1 whole chicken	salt and pepper to taste
1 small onion, cut up	3 sprigs parsley
3 or 4 medium tomatoes	6 flour tortillas
1 pinch thyme	1 large or medium avocado

Simmer chicken with onion, salt, pepper, thyme, parsley, and tomatoes in 9-inch Calphalon sauteuse till meat comes away from bones. (About one hour.) Drain and cool chicken, then remove skin and bones neatly so that you have fairly large pieces of meat to work with. Divide meat into six portions and lay each across center of tortillas. Top chicken with onions and tomato (no skins) strained from broth and roll outside edges inward to form a cylinder. Chalupas may be served at room temperature or warmed in medium oven, but just before serving top each one with a tablespoonful of puréed avocado.

NOTE: Leftover broth and chicken skin may be put through blender to make a rich soup stock

Oven-Barbecued Chicken

A savory method for keeping chicken tender — with a last-minute pass under the broiler to produce the heat-seared flavor of open-pit barbecuing.

1 large fryer, cut up
3 medium tomatoes
1 teaspoon worcestershire sauce
1 tablespoon brown sugar
3 tablespoons tarragon vinegar
1 teaspoon salt
1 teaspoon course ground pepper
2 tablespoons Maggi Seasoning

Arrange chicken pieces on flat baking tray and start them on bottom shelf of oven at 350° F. Puree tomatoes in blender and strain. Add all other ingredients to strained puree and mix thoroughly. Pour sauce evenly over chicken and continue baking for 30 minutes or till chicken is tender. Then pass under broiler for 5 minutes or till sauce becomes a deep brown. Serve in deep dish or Calphalon sauteuse.

Hawaiian Chicken

1 fryer, cut up
POLYNESIAN SAUCE (see recipe under SAUCES)

Arrange chicken in flat baking tray and begin baking as in OVEN-BARBECUED CHICKEN, on lowest shelf of oven at 350° F. Follow recipe for POLYNESIAN SAUCE and pour evenly over chicken. Continue baking to about 30 minutes total or till meat next to breastbone is tender.

Chicken Paprika

1 large broiler or fryer
1 teaspoon paprika (must be very fresh)
3/4 teaspoon salt
1/2 teaspoon sugar
1/8 teaspoon white pepper

Arrange pieces on baking sheet. In small bowl blend seasonings together and sprinkle evenly over chicken. Bake in hot over (400° F.) for 35 minutes, then turn pieces and bake 10 to 15 minutes longer.

Poulet Basquais
(Basque Chicken in Tomato Juice)

Like *CHINESE CHICKEN*, this recipe is one of the purest examples of the New Cuisine: light, simple ingredients, combined in a highly original flavor.

1 large fryer, in small pieces
1/4 cup peanut oil
1/4 cup chopped onion
1/8 cup chopped green pepper
1 pinch (or more if desired) powdered garlic
1/2 cup chopped carrots
1/2 cup chopped celery with leaves
2 cups puréed tomatoes, strained
OR — 1½ cup tomato juice

Brown chicken in oil, using your 9-inch Calphalon sauteuse. Remove pieces and saute onion, peppers, and garlic in remaining oil. Return chicken to pan and add carrots, celery, and tomato juice, pouring them over chicken. Simmer covered for about one hour. Just before serving, top with thinly sliced stuffed olives or grated parsley.

Chicken Galantine
(Chicken in Aspic)

A Galantine is a beautiful way to serve *POULE AU POT* or *POULET BASQUAIS* in hot weather. It can be prepared ahead in the cool of the day, and grows more savory during chilling.

Follow recipe for either:
  POULE AU POT or POULET BASQUAIS
  2 packets unflavored gelatine

Remove skin and bones from chicken and cut meat into thin slices. Strain broth and chill in refrigerator till slightly "set." (For a firmer galantine, you may want to add one more packet of unflavored gelatin. Dissolve this according to directions and stir into hot strained broth before chilling.) when broth begins to set but is not yet firm, brush it onto sides and bottom of chilled gelatin mold or 12-inch Calphalon omelet pan, and rechill pan till gelatin is as firm as possible. Then lay chicken pieces into mold and pour half-set broth over it, spreading evenly, and chill for several hours.

TO UNMOLD — Pass mold quickly over pan of warm water and towel it dry. Then lay large plate or serving platter upside down over top of mold, and invert so that galantine comes neatly out of mold. If you wish, you can serve galantine under a mayonnaise mask. Use the recipe suggested for *EGGS MAYONNAISE.*

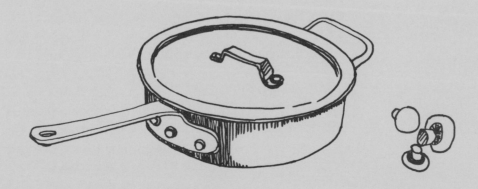

Fish
and
Seafood

CHAPTER SIX

FISH and SEAFOOD

When a recipe calls for fresh fish or seafood, the advice is not to be taken lightly. I know that in the past many markets have been able to sell partly or wholly thawed frozen fish as "fresh" — but the consumer's movement has done much to end this deceit. When a fish is frozen, the moisture in it expands, breaking apart the tissues that contain it. Therefore a thawed fish will be somewhat limp and subject to much more rapid spoilage. Whether the fish you buy is labeled "FRESH" or "FRESH FROZEN AND THAWED," it's a good idea to wash it thoroughly in cold water before refrigerating and then again before using. Some of the following recipes can be used with thawed or even canned fish and seafood (the flavor will be less delicate, more intense.) In these recipes, look for specific recommendations.

Poached Fish

"Poaching" a fish is neither steaming nor boiling, but somewhere in between. The following recipe is recommended for all kinds of fresh fish, as well as for shrimp, scallops, mussels, lobster, langouste (or crayfish), and even skate.

1 thin slice onion
1 bayleaf
1 celery stalk with leaves
1 slice lemon
1/2 teaspoon salt
1 dash white pepper
2 cups water

Place these ingredients in a pan just large enough to accommodate fish or seafood to be poached. (A Calphalon sauteuse is ideal.) Bring water to a boil, turn down heat and simmer covered for 15 minutes. Add fish or seafood and simmer at lowest heat possible for 15 minutes more. Serve at once, or see any of the following recipes for special sauces and garnishes.

Coquilles St. Jacques
(French-Style Scallops Baked in Individual Shells)

This dish — like its Spanish cousin *VIEIRAS a la GALLEGA* — has a lovely history, dating from the Middle Ages. Pilgrims to the Shrine of St. James, in northern Spain, used to walk there from Paris, a a distance of 900 miles. As part of their "camping equipment," they carried three scallop shells: one to use for drinking, one as a plate, the third to "spoon" their food. The route they walked was never far from the sea, so we know that scallops must have formed an important staple. The Roman name for the saint was Iacobus, which the French evolved to Jacques and the Spanish to Iago and Diego.

The ideal ingredient for this recipe is fresh bay scallops, a true shellfish. But you may also use "deep sea scallops," a slightly coarser counterfeit cut from the flesh of various white saltwater fish.

> 1 pound or more scallops, poached according to
>   preceding recipe
> 2 cups NEW CUISINE WHITE SAUCE (see recipe)
> 1 cup fresh white button mushrooms
> 1/2 cup medium sherry
> 1/2 cup grated mild white cheddar or jack cheese
> 1 cub bread crumbs
> 1/4 cup melted unsalted butter

Poach scallops according to recipe. If using "deep sea scallops," which are larger, divide into quarters. Remove scallops from poaching pan and arrange on baking shells — one shell for each person to be served. Strain liquor left from poaching and blend into *NEW CUISINE WHITE SAUCE*. Remove sauce from heat but keep it warm. Wash, blot dry, and slice mushrooms into thin vertical slices. Heat a very small amount of fresh olive or peanut oil, or unsalted butter, in Calphalon butter warmer and add mushrooms. Saute them quickly, turning them constantly with a fork till edges turn golden. At highest heat, begin adding sherry, a few drips at a time, letting the alcohol steam away without being absorbed by mushrooms. When mushrooms are golden and glazed, distribute them in an even layer over scallops in baking shells. Pour white sauce over each shell. Rinse out Calphalon butter warmer and melt butter at low heat. Toss bread crumbs in melted butter and then grated cheese. Divide this topping over each baking shell. Just before serving, pass shells under broiler for 5 minutes to reheat and turn topping golden brown.

Vieiras a la Gallega
(Spanish Scallops)

This delightful dish deserves to be better known — if only because it's easier to prepare. Popular today at the "other" end of the St. James trail — the shrine of Santiago de Compostela in the Spanish province of Galicia — it takes its special flavor not from cheese but from Serrano ham, a Spanish delicacy like Prosciutto, York, or any lean domestic ham. Vieiras are often served in a sauteuse rather than shells.

1 pound or more fresh scallops
1/2 pound finely chopped Serrano ham (see above)
1 cup grated bread crumbs, either stale or toasted
1/2 cup very fresh olive oil
1 clove garlic
OR — 1 dash powdered garlic
2 tablespoons finely grated parsley
1/4 teaspoon ground white pepper

Wash scallops and blot dry. If using "deep sea scallops" cut them into quarters. In Calphalon butter warmer, lightly saute onion, ham, garlic, parsley, and bread crumbs in oil. Arrange scallops in Calphalon sauteuse and season with a mixture of salt, pepper, and cold olive oil. Put them under broiler for two minutes. Remove, cover them with crumb mixture — or *sofrito* — and pass them under broiler again for about three minutes. Serve at once.

Cold Prawns in Their Shells

For alfresco dinners, luncheons, and picnics it would be hard to imagine a simpler yet more elegant dish.

1 pound or more large prawns, poached
according to recipe for POACHED FISH
2 (or more) cups Mayonnaise (see recipe)

Poach shrimp according to recipe, drain thoroughly, and chill. Serve in shells on lettuce bed, accompanied by saucedish of cold mayonnaise. Allow 1/4 pound of prawns for each person, and accompany with crusty oven-warmed homemade or French bread, butter, and chilled dry cider or chablis wine.

NOTE: Liquor in which prawns were poached can be saved for *MEDITERRANEAN FISH SOUP* (see recipe) or blended — strained — with canned jellied consomme for another superb hot-weather menu offering.

Seviche Peruano
(Peruvian "Cold-Cooked" Whitefish)

Almost everyone who visits the Latin American tropics marvels at the delicacy of this simple fish recipe, "cooked" without heat. According to my friends Rosita and Carlitos, the secret lies in using absolutely fresh and fine-textured fish. The "cooking" takes place with the enzyme action of the lime juice and must be ended at just the right moment.

*1 fillet per person of boneless, fine-textured
    white fish — sole, butterfish, mahi-mahi,
    perch, etc.*
1/4 cup fresh strained lime juice
1 pinch each: salt, cayenne, onion powder

Arrange fillets on serving platter layered with fresh lettuce leaves. Stir seasonings into lime juice and spread evenly over fillets. Chill fish overnight or at least four hours before serving.

Hot Crab Meat Salad

This recipe is pure Americana. It defies all rules and categories, but is too delicious to ignore. It makes an indeal fish course but could also serve as hors d'ouvre, luncheon entree, or buffet dish. Either fresh or canned crab will work, but unless you cooked the crab yourself, be sure to wash and blot it dry before using.

1/2 pound cooked crab
OR — 8 ounces canned crab meat (see above)
1½ cups whole milk
1/2 cup fresh bread crumbs
1 cup chopped celery
2 beaten egg yolks
1/2 teaspoon salt
1/2 teaspoon paprika
1/2 teaspoon Worcestershire sauce
1/2 cup mayonnaise
1 tablespoon lemon juice
2 egg whites, beaten stiff
1 cup buttered corn flakes

Flake crab into 9-inch Calphalon sauteuse and mix in all other ingredients except egg whites and corn flakes. Fold in egg whites, top with corn flakes. Bake 30 minutes at 350° F.

Baked Fruits of The Sea

Though this is one of my favorite recipes, I rarely make it the same way twice. Its contents usually depend on the "catch of the day" and the contents of the cupboard. The general rule is that it contains at least one kind of fish, one variety of seafood, plus mushrooms, cheese, and white sauce.

1 pound sole, turbot, or boneless fresh fish
1/2 pound shrimp, crab, or scallops
  (canned may be used)
2 cups NEW CUISINE WHITE SAUCE (see recipe)
1 cup washed, sliced fresh mushrooms
1/2 cup buttered breadcrumbs
1/2 cup grated gruyere or swiss cheese

Poach fish according to recipe, drain, and layer in bottom of oiled 9-inch Calphalon sauteuse. Strain broth left from poaching and stir into 2 cups *NEW CUISINE WHITE SAUCE.* Pour half of sauce over fish, add layer of mushrooms, then a third layer of seafood. Cover with remaining sauce and top with breadcrumbs and cheese. Bake 20 minutes at medium heat — 350° F. — and serve.

Baked Sole in Cheese Sauce

2 pounds fillet of sole (you may substitute turbot or boneless butterfish)
1 cup (about half of recipe) NEW CUISINE WHITE SAUCE
2½ cups grated white cheddar or jack cheese

Arrange fillets in bottom of greased Calphalon sauteuse. Make white sauce according to recipe and gradually stir in cheese till smooth. Pour mixture evenly over fish and bake in medium oven (350° F.) for 20 minutes or till tender. Garnish with grated parsley and lemon wedges, and serve at once.

Lox
(Cold Preserved Salmon)

During the short season for fresh salmon, prices are appealing but not every family can eat salmon every day. My friend Aileene developed this delightful recipe for lengthening the season.

2¼ pounds fresh salmon in center-cut fillets
1 teaspoon hickory-smoked seasoning
8 teaspoons pickling salt   2 tablespoons sugar

Mix dry ingredients and coat salmon on both sides and ends. Sprinkle remainder in the bottom of a glass baking dish large enough to hold salmon in single layer. Cover salmon with plastic wrap and refrigerate for one week or more. To serve, slice cold fillets very thin, top with grated parsley and accompany with lemon wedges.

Sole Buerre Noir
(Sole in Black Butter)

This classic recipe can be adapted to any fine fish. The flavor comes through best if you use unsalted butter and it should be watched carefully till it reaches a deep brown shade rather than black.

1 small fillet of sole per person
1/2 cup unsalted butter
1/4 cup capers, drained

Poach fish according to recipe. During poaching heat butter in Calphalon butter warmer. Remove from heat when thoroughly brown but not burnt. Lift fish carefully from pan and lay on pre-warmed serving tray. Stir capers into butter, then pour butter evenly over fish. Serve at once.

NOTE: Liquor from poaching may be saved for use in fish soup. Or it can be strained, mixed with unflavored gelatine, and used as a galantine for canned salmon. (See recipe for *CHICKEN GALANTINE.*)

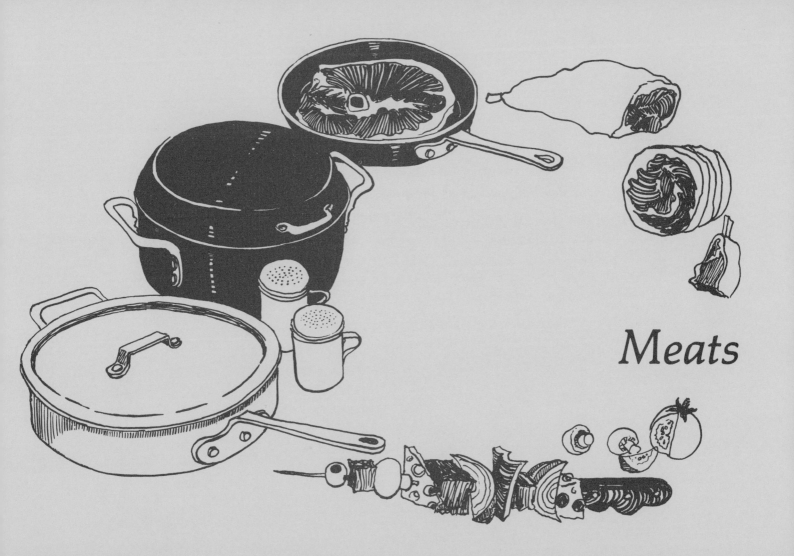

Meats

CHAPTER SEVEN

MEATS

By tradition, meat has long served as the husky part of every meal. The New Cuisine takes a slightly different approach. Now meat is also a flavoring, a balancer. The following recipes are meant for meat-eaters with hearty appetites — but sometimes the emphasis falls on other, lighter ingredients.

Stuffed Flank Steak

Unless your butcher is a good friend, it's possible you've never discovered how good, how versatile, a fresh flank steak can be. I've tried the following recipe using top round steak — which also works — but nothing excels the exquisite cut from the flank. You may find it expensive — but a large cut serves 6 to 8 persons.

> *1 large flank steak (1½ pounds or more)*
> *2 cups Lemon Rice or Fried Brown Rice (see recipe under*
> *   POTATOES, RICE and NOODLES)*
> *3 tablespoons Maggi Seasoning*
> *1 pinch powdered garlic*

Rub Maggi seasoning and garlic powder into steak 1/2-hour before cooking. Prepare rice according to recipe. Sear fat side of steak on French grill pan or under broiler till fat turns black. Remove from heat, spread hot rice stuffing across cooked side of steak and roll ends around stuffing. Fasten with skewer. Turn roll, skewer side down, rub topside with butter or oil, and place under broiler for 15 minutes. Serve at once on carving tray and slice like a roast for individual servings.

Roulade of Beef

A minature version of *STUFFED FLANK STEAK*, *Roulade of Beef* is my own recourse whenever meat prices soar. From an average beef rump roast, your butcher can make 20 to 30 thin slices of meat — each to be stuffed and broiled as an individual serving. If meat is sliced very thin, you may want to top with a spoonful of heated beef consomme or reconstituted beef bouillon to prevent dryness.

2 thin slices beef rump roast per person
1 tablespoon Lemon Rice or Fried Brown Rice per serving (see recipe)
2 tablespoons Maggi seasoning
1 pinch powdered garlic

Prepare rice according to recipe and place 1 tablespoon in center of each slice of beef. Roll up slice, fasten with toothpick, and lay rolls seam downward in large Calphalon omelet pan or sauteuse. Sprinkle tops of roulades with Maggi Seasoning, garlic, and a dash of oil if meat is lean. Pass under broiler for 5 minutes and serve at once in pan.

Piccadillo Cubano
(Cuban Ground Beef Casserole)

Roughly translated, "piccadillo" means a homely little something, all chopped up. Obviously, the person who named this dish would hesitate to serve it to visiting royalty — which may partly explain why it's no fun to be king!

1½ pounds lean ground beef
2 medium onions
2 green bell peppers
1 medium-size jar stuffed olives (save juice)
1 cup seedless raisins
4 puréed strained tomatoes
OR — 6 ounces canned tomato sauce
4 tablespoons olive or peanut oil

Half of juice strained from olives
1/4 teaspoon oregano
1/2 teaspoon salt
1/4 teaspoon ground pepper
1/2 teaspoon garlic powder
1/2 teaspoon celery salt
1/4 teaspoon paprika

Brown meat lightly in 9-inch Calphalon sauteuse, turning frequently with fork. Drain and remove from pan. Add oil and saute onions and peppers. Stir in all ingredients except meat, raisins, and olives. When thoroughly blended, slice olives and add remaining ingredients, cooking slowly — with cover — for about 40 minutes.

Piccadillo should be served hot and accompanied with steamed rice.

Sweetbreads Chez Moi

There are many ways to prepare sweetbreads. I recently found a recipe that called for dipping them into a very thin egg batter, so that they could easily pass for mock abalone steak. Needless to say, this dish was popular among those who like abalone better than sweetbreads — and the following recipe is also something of a compromise. If the meat doesn't win you over, the mushrooms are bound to!

1½ to 2 pounds sweetbreads
1 pound fresh white button mushrooms
1 bay leaf
1 slice fresh lemon
1 slice of onion
1 dash each: salt, white pepper, garlic powder
1/2 cup white port wine
2 tablespoons unsalted butter
1-2 cups NEW CUISINE WHITE SAUCE (see recipe)

Wash sweetbreads in cold water, removing as much of the white membrane as possible. Set them simmering in Calphalon sauteuse, along with 2 cups water, bay leaf, onion, lemon, salt, pepper, and garlic, for 15 to 20 minutes, or till tender. Remove sweetbreads to cool and strain broth. Prepare *NEW CUISINE WHITE SAUCE* using broth instead of water (though you may have to add water to complete measurements). Rinse and dry sauteuse, melt butter in it, and saute mushrooms which you have rinsed and carefully blotted dry. When mushrooms turn golden, start pouring wine, a few drops at a time, into sauteuse. Do not add more wine till previous addition has stopped steaming. When all the wine has been scalded, turn off heat and remove the last of the white membranes from sweetbreads. Slice them into small pieces, scatter them over mushrooms, and stir sauce into pan, reheating at very low heat. Serve in sauteuse or casserole, topped with fresh grated parsley, and accompanied with Lemon Rice (see recipe) or Small Parsleyed New Potatoes.

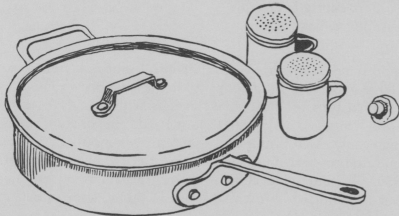

Pork Chops Lorraine

Ideally this recipe should be used with a large, lean tenderloin of pork — a cut that's easier to come by in France than in the United States. But through the years I have adapted it to small, center-cut pork chops — and the method is now a family favorite.

4 thick pork chops (or 1 per person)
1/2 cup fine bread crumbs, lightly salted and peppered
2 tablespoons finely chopped chives
2 tablespoons grated fresh parsley
1 dash garlic powder
1/2 cup chicken or veal stock, or reconstituted bouillon crystals
2 tablespoons unsalted butter
1 tablespoon white vinegar

Trim fat and bones from chops. Rub fat into Calphalon omelet pan (must be large enough to hold chops in one layer). Brown chops on both sides, then turn off heat. Cover chops with a layer of bread crumbs. Mix chives, parsley and garlic; add to bread crumbs, distributing evenly. Melt butter and spoon it over chops. Pass chops under broiler to brown them, then add stock to pan, turn down oven heat to 350° F., and bake chops covered for about 50 minutes. Uncover for 10 minutes to brown meat again. Stir vinegar into sauce and serve at once.

Bockwurst

Despite the fact that this beautiful veal sausage comes to us from a cold climate, I've discovered that its easy cooking and gentle piquancy are very welcome on hot summer evenings, as well as nippy autumn nights.

4 bockwurst sausages (or at least one per person)
1 stick cinnamon
1/2 cup strained cider or apple juice

Use Calphalon sauteuse which will barely accommodate sausages and cover bottom with cider and cinnamon. If necessary, add water to bring level to about 1/4 inch and break cinnamon stick into pieces to distribute flavor. Simmer covered at lowest possible heat for 15 minutes, adding either more cider or water if necessary. Rinse sausages and blot thoroughly dry, then add to pan. Continue simmering under cover, but check occasionally to make sure sausages do not expand to the point of bursting their skins. This will probably take about 10 minutes. Bockwurst may be kept warm till serving time, then topped with grated parsley and accompanied by hot or cold potato salad, sauerkraut or tomatoes vinaigrette.

Shepherd's Pie
(No-Crust Meat Tart)

By tradition this dish is made with ground cooked lamb, usually leftovers from a roast "joint," as they say in England. However, it works just as well with any precooked meat — beef, chicken, veal, pork, ham, or some combination. The secret lies in cooking it before grinding, so that it doesn't "steam" in its own juices.

1 to 2 pounds cooked meat
1 or 2 slices fresh bread
2 tablespoons Maggi seasoning

1 cup fresh sliced mushrooms
2-3 small tomatoes
2 cups (approximately) mashed potatoes

Put meat through grinder, removing tendons, skin, and any other part which will not pass through grinder with ease. Grind bread at the last to force the last bit of meat through openings. Toss meat with Maggi seasoning to blend mixture thoroughly. Slice mushrooms and toss them with the meat if meat has some amount of fat in it. (If not you can either arrange fresh mushroom slices in a layer on top of meat or saute them in butter and sherry.) Wash, dry, and remove stem end from tomatoes. Slice them thinly and arrange in a layer on top of meat or spread them as a "crust" or top layer to your pie. For elegance, you can also put mashed potatoes through a cooky press, covering the top of your "pie" with rosettes or some pretty holiday motif. Bake pie in medium oven (350° F.) or till potatoes begin to turn golden brown. Serve while hot.

Classic Baked Ham

The following recipe is best with either fresh cured or canned ham — but can also be used on any ham that's been smoked, though the flavor will be less subtle.

> *1 medium size ham, 3 or more pounds*
> *1 8-ounce can pineapple rings plus juice*
> *1/4 cup prepared mustard*
> *1/4 cup brown sugar*
> *6 dried cloves (approximately)*
> *6 maraschino cherries*

Place ham in 9-inch Calphalon sauteuse or baking pan, fattest side up if canned. Score skin diagonally in diamond pattern if using fresh ham. Drain pineapple rings and mix juice with mustard and brown sugar. Lay rings on top of ham, place cherries in center, and fasten each one with spike of clove. Pour mustard sauce over top and bake 1 hour at 350° F., basting frequently. Serve on carving platter.

Beef Strudel with Mushroom Sauce

This is another recipe born to glorify leftover cooked meat. I first tried it with beef, but later found it a marvelous way to deal with chicken, pork, and ham, as well.

1 to 2 pounds cooked meat
1 cup cooked rice — any method
1/4 cup melted butter
2 tablespoons peanut oil
2 tablespoons Maggi Seasoning
3 leaves of Greek fila dough*
1 cup fresh white mushrooms
1/2 cup white port wine
2 tablespoons cornstarch
1 cup bouillon

Put meat through grinder, using all the fat but cutting away those parts which will not pass through easily. Toss meat with rice, Maggi Seasoning, and lay in center of first leaf of fila dough. Quickly roll dough around meat and seal ends to form a log-shaped roll and coat roll with mixture of melted butter and oil. Place roll in center of second leaf and repeat, brushing oil and butter onto both sides of leaf.

Use third leaf the same way, tucking in ends, and brushing on butter-oil mixture till outside of strudel is thoroughly coated. Bake at 350° F. for 40 minutes or till strudel is golden brown. During baking, prepare sauce as follows:

Wash mushrooms, blot thoroughly dry, and slice thin. Saute them till edges turn light brown in butter or oil. Add wine, a few drips at a time till sauce at bottom of pan turns shiny and bubbles without steaming. Turn off heat and remove mushrooms, draining away as much sauce as possible. Mix corn starch with 1 cup bouillon and add slowly to sauce in pan, blending thoroughly. Reheat till sauce thickens, then remove from heat. Add salt if needed and stir in mushrooms. Serve strudel on carving tray, topped with mushroom sauce, and slice like roast beef.

* Available in frozen food counter at many supermarkets

Meatballs Joanna

When Joanna was eight and first learning to cook, she kept falling in love with the most complicated of recipes. After much refinement, she came up with the following concoction which cuts the original number of ingredients by half and intensifies the flavor by two.

1 pound ground beef
1 cup fresh bread crumbs
4 sprigs chopped parsley
1 tablespoon Maggi Seasoning
1 dash each: salt, pepper, Angostura bitters
1/8 cup chopped chives
1 tablespoon lemon juice
5 tablespoons bouillon crystals
1 cup water
1/2 cup concentrated or condensed milk
2 teaspoons cornstarch

With minimum of handling, mix meat, bread crumbs, parsley, Maggi seasoning, salt, pepper, lemon juice and bitters in bowl, and roll into balls one inch in diameter. In 9-inch Calphalon sauteuse bring water, chives, and bouillon crystals to boil, lower heat, and simmer 15 minutes. Add meatballs, simmering 15 minutes more. Remove meatballs. Blend cornstarch and milk, add gradually to pan, and stir gently till sauce thickens. Salt and pepper to taste, then return meatballs to sauteuse, or serve on platter covered with sauce and garnished with grated parsley.

Giblets Marie

In England, chicken giblets — and in fact the organic parts of all meat — are called "offal," which to many Americans sounds "awful." The following recipe for *Giblets Marie* has decided many a Yankee heart that chicken "offal" can taste terrific!

1 pound or more chicken giblets
1 cup chicken stock or reconstituted bouillon
1/4 cup melted butter
1/4 cup peanut oil
1 pinch each: salt, pepper, paprika, garlic powder

Wash giblets and blot dry. Simmer them in Calphalon sauteuse with stock till tender, about 15 minutes. Drain and spread in Calhalon omelet pan or ovenproof baking dish. Stir seasonings into butter/oil mixture and pour evenly over giblets. Broil 5 minutes, turn, and broil 3 minutes more. Serve with topping of grated parsley, or make a sauce with leftover broth according to recipe for *NEW CUISINE WHITE SAUCE.*

Leg of Lamb Muscadet

"But how does one roast a leg of lamb without nutmeg?" a friend from Bordeau asked me. The answer seemed obvious at first — but after trying her recipe, I couldn't agree more heartily.

1 small leg of lamb, 3 to 4 pounds
1 dash each: Maggi seasoning, salt pepper,
garlic powder, ground nutmeg.

If lamb is covered with a heavy outer membrane — the fell — score it crosswise so that seasonings will penetrate into fat but not into the meat itself. Rub seasonings into fell in the order listed, nutmeg last. Roast room-temperature lamb at very low heat to prevent shrinkage, about 250° F. for about 40 minutes per pound, or use a meat thermometer. Serve with Mint Sauce (see recipe) and Parsleyed Potatoes.

Chateaubriand Steak Garni

It's hard to improve on a simple London broil steak — but the first time I tried *Chateaubriand Garni* — with its five fresh-steamed garden vegetables drenched in a sauce of melted butter and juice from the steak, I couldn't decide whether I preferred the meat-flavored vegetables or the vegetable-savored steak. Maybe you can decide.

1 medium London broil steak, 2 to 3 pounds
2 cups each: diced carrots, celery, zucchini
*   squash, cherry tomatoes, green beans*
2 tablespoons melted butter
1 tablespoon peanut oil
1 tablespoon Maggi seasoning
1 pinch each: salt, pepper, garlic powder

Mix butter and oil and brush mixture over both sides of steak. Rub in Maggi and seasonings, and let seasoned steak warm to room temperature, about one hour. Prepare vegetables and arrange them separately around edges of large (12 inches or more) Calphalon omelet pan. Salt vegetables lightly and add just enough water to cover bottom of pan. Cover pan, place on bottom shelf of oven, and turn oven to *broil.* After 15 minutes remove pan. Spoon liquid over vegetables and place steak in pan. Pour remaining marinade over vegetables and pass pan under broiler uncovered for 15 minutes more. If steak is not yet brown, baste vegetables again, pass under broiler for 3 minutes more, and serve at once in pan or transfer all to carving board.

Parisian Steak

Friends and family call this "Butterball Steak." Though portions are small — one top grade round steak serves six people — no one has yet complained of leaving the table hungry.

1 thick-cut top grade round steak
6 tablespoons unsalted whipped butter
2 tablespoons peanut oil
2 tablespoons Maggi seasoning
1 pinch powdered garlic

Rub oil into lean part of steak, avoiding bone and fat, then rub Maggi Seasoning into oil. Coat fat with garlic, and set steak aside for at least one hour to season and bring to room temperature. Meanwhile, spoon butter into 6 balls, roll in parsley and refrigerate till serving. Just before mealtime, pass steak under preheated broiler for 5 minutes, turn, and broil 2 minutes longer. Lay steak on preheated carving tray, arrange butterballs on top, and carve separate servings at table. Areas around bone will be rarest.

Ham en Gelée

Here is a cold dish, ideal for summer and perfect for finishing off a holiday ham, at luncheon, brunch, or buffet.

2 cups cooked, diced ham
1 cup stuffed olives
4 packets unflavored powdered gelatin
2 tablespoons lemon juice
2 cups water

Drain, wash, and slice olives. Soften gelatin in lemon juice and stir into boiling water. Chill small Calphalon omelet pan or gelatin mold and cool gelatin mixture in refrigerator. When mold is cold, coat with gelatin mixture, and return to refrigerator to set. Toss olive slices with ham and spread mixture in coated mold. Pour gelatin mixture over all and refrigerate at least one hour more. To remove *Ham en Gelee* from mold, pass mold over pan of warm water and invert serving platter over top of mold. Turn mold upside down. *Gelee* should come out clean — but if it doesn't, repeat warm water process. *Ham en Gelee* can be served garnished with asparagus tips and water chestnuts, or with a mayonnaise mask suggested in the recipe for *EGGS MAYONNAISE.*

Dolmathes
(Meat-Stuffed Grape or Cabbage Leaves)

1 pound lean ground beef
1 small chopped tomato
1 onion, chopped fine
2 fresh mint leaves, chopped fine
1 pinch garlic powder
1/2 teaspoon salt
1 pinch ground white pepper
1/2 cup water
1/8 cup long-grain white rice
1 jar preserved grape leaves
OR — 3 to 4 dozen fresh grape leaves
OR — 2 small heads green cabbage
1½ cups beef stock or bouillon
3 tablespoons peanut oil
3 egg yolks
1/8 cup fresh lemon juice

These meat-stuffed leaves are served with a drenching of lemon sauce — sometimes as a side dish with roast lamb but often and justifiably as a main course.

Drop meat in small pieces into 12-inch Calphalon omelet pan, and toss at low heat, gradually adding onion. If meat sticks to pan, add a little oil. When mixture begins to brown, stir in mint, salt, pepper, tomato, garlic, and water. Simmer covered for 1/2 hour, then stir in rice and turn off flame or remove from heat. If using preserved grape leaves, rinse and drain in warm water. Fresh grape or cabbage leaves should be tenderized quickly in boiling salted water, then drained dry. Fill each leaf with 1 tablespoonful meat mixture and wrap edges around filling. Rinse out omelet pan, wipe dry, and arrange leaves folded side downward in pan. Stir oil into stock and pour over leaves. Simmer covered for about an hour. Meanwhile beat together egg yolks and lemon juice, in Calphalon butter warmer. When leaves are cooked, whisk broth into egg mixture and warm over lowest possible heat till sauce begins to thicken. Pour over leaves and serve at once.

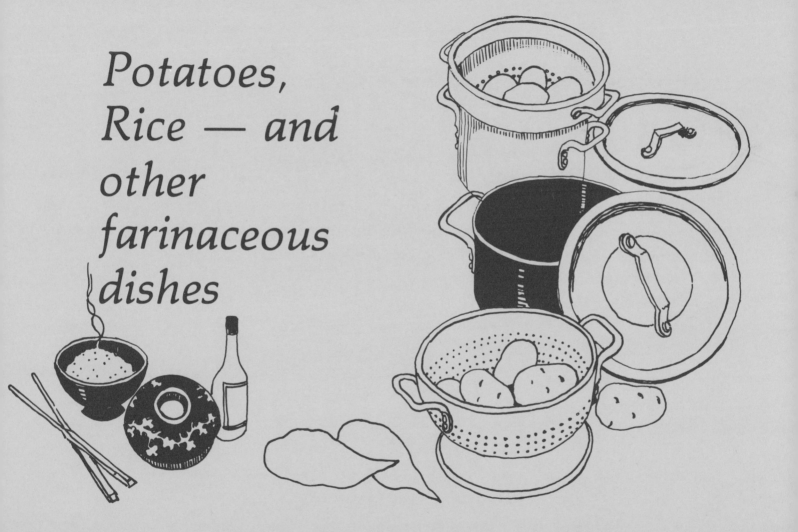

CHAPTER EIGHT

Potatoes, Rice — and other farinaceous dishes

POTATOES, RICE
— and other farinaceous dishes

For a long time, nutrition-oriented cooks have regarded starchy dishes like potatoes as a needless fillip — like the tough parsley stem that decorates many a restaurant steak. The following recipes are meant for small servings — but as for flavor, they stand on their own.

Parsleyed New Potatoes

Tiny white new potatoes are the classic ingredient for this recipe — but I confess that small red potatoes cut in halves or even quarters taste better than they have any right to.

2 new potatoes per person
OR — 1 red potato each, halved
2 sprigs fresh mint
1 teaspoon salt
Water to barely cover potatoes
OR — 2 cups in bottom of Calphalon steamer
3 tablespoons melted butter
3 tablespoons peanut oil
1 tablespoon fresh grated parsley

Wash potatoes, and remove eyes. Set mint, salt and water to boil in Calphalon sauteuse. Add potatoes and cook at lowest possible heat till tender, about 20 minutes. Meantime, melt butter and stir in oil. When potatoes are done, arrange on serving dish or drain water and mint from sauteuse. Spoon butter mixture over potatoes and sprinkle parsley overall.

Fried Brown Rice

This recipe came to me from a friend who was living on a vegetarian diet while conducting backpack trips through California's rugged Trinity Alps. After a few spoonfuls of his *Fried Brown Rice*, I stopped wondering where he got his stamina.

1 cup brown rice, unwashed
2½ cups water
1 teaspoon salt
1 tablespoon soy sauce
2 tablespoons Maggi Seasoning
1/2 cup each: finely chopped peeled carrots, celery,
*   green pepper, and onions*
1 dash each: ground black pepper, dried oregano
2 tablespoons peanut oil

Heat oil in Calphalon, then add all ingredients except water and rice. Toss at medium heat for 5 minutes, then add rice slowly and continue tossing. When all ingredients are thoroughly blended, add water. Cover and simmer at lowest heat possible for 45 minutes or till rice is tender. Serve with topping of grated parsley or toasted sesame seeds.

New Cuisine Steamed Rice

For those who like "just plain rice," this recipe is a dish to dream on. Its bland, firm texture makes a perfect foil for piquant dishes like *PICADILLO CUBANO*, and subtle ones too, like *COQ aux CORINTHES* or *BAKED SOLE in CHEESE SAUCE* (see recipes).

> 1 cup long-grained white rice, unwashed
> 6 cups water
> 2 teaspoons salt

Put water and salt in bottom of Calphalon vegetable steamer, cover and bring to boil. Insert steamer top, so that water which folows in covers perforated bottom. While salted water is still at low boil, pour in rice a few grains at a time to maintain heat. Cover and cook for 5 minutes. Stir once and turn off heat, leaving rice covered for one hour or till grains swell to desired texture. Just before serving you may stir in 2 tablespoons melted unsalted butter or 2 tablespoons peanut oil.

Lemon Rice

1 cup unwashed long-grain white rice
2 tablespoons peanut oil
1¾ cups white stock or reconstituted chicken bouillon
Juice from 1 fresh medium lemon
(optional — 1/2 teaspoon grated lemon peel, fine)
1 tablespoon fine-chopped fresh parsley
2 tablespoons melted unsalted butter

Warm oil slowly in Calphalon sauteuse, and add rice a few grains at a time till coated but not browned in oil. Add stock and simmer covered till all moisture is taken up — about 20 to 30 minutes. If rice becomes too dry before tender, add a little water, about 1/4 cup. When grains have swelled to capacity, uncover and shake pan to separate. Toss with melted butter till thoroughly blended, then stir in lemon and parsley. Serve as soon as possible.

Mistress Mary's Herbed Yorkshire Pudding

My English in-laws are so celebrated for their perfect Yorkshire puddings that for years I was terrified of trying one on my own. The following recipe came to me by way of a fellow midwesterner — along with a large dose of courage. I am happy to report that the latter is completely unnecessary. By tradition, Yorkshire pudding accompanies roast beef, and takes its special flavor from the drippings.

Beef drippings
3 eggs
1¼ cups milk
1 cup enriched flour
1 teaspoon salt
1 tablespoon fresh grated parsley
1/4 teaspoon each: dried rosemary and thyme

During last 10 minutes of roasting meat, prepare batter as follows. Beat eggs till fluffy. Measure sifted flour, and add with other ingredients to eggs. Mix just enough to make batter smooth. Remove roast from oven and raise heat to 450° F. Spoon hot drippings from roasting pan — 1½ tablespoons for each individual glass baking cup, or section of muffin tin. Add batter to half-fill each cup and bake for 15 minutes. Then reduce heat to 350° F. and bake 10 to 15 minutes more, till puddings are puffy and golden brown. Serve as soon as possible.

Vegetables

CHAPTER NINE

VEGETABLES

Vegetables are the NEW CUISINE'S crowning glory. If you've never steamed vegetables before, your CALPHALON steamer is bound to make you feel you've invented a rainbow of flavors. But most of the following recipes will also work by using minimal amounts of water in any CALPHALON pan with a well-fitted lid.

Buttered Noodle Casserole

This rather hearty dish is ideal as a partner to any slender meat course — cold sliced roast beef, boiled ham, or *PORK CHOPS LORRAINE* (see recipe).

2 cups egg noodles
1 cup chopped celery
2 cups stock or reconstituted bouillon crystals
1 tablespoon melted butter
1 tablespoon peanut oil
1 cup stale bread crumbs

Slowly simmer stock in Calphalon sauteuse. When just boiling add celery and noodles slowly and cook uncovered till noodles are tender. In Calphalon butter warmer melt butter, stir in oil, and toss bread crumbs. Drain any excess moisture from noodles and toss with a very small amount of oil to separate. Top noodles with crumb mixture and pass under broiler to brown, no more than 3 minutes. Serve at once.

Eggplant Parmagiano

1 medium ripe eggplant
1/4 cup each: finely chopped onions, celery, green peppers
2 tablespoons peanut oil
2 medium tomatoes
1/2 cup grated parmesan cheese
OR — 1/2 cup grated sharp gruyere
1 dash each: garlic powder, salt, ground black pepper

Wash, dry, and slice eggplant in half-inch cross sections, five to eight slices. Blanch quickly in Calphalon steamer (or large omelet pan) till slices are barely transparent around skin edge. Drain and place evenly on baking sheet. Heat oil in Calphalon butter warmer and saute onions, celery, and green peppers. Spoon these over eggplant slices. Make second layer with grated cheese. Puree tomatoes in blender. Strain out seeds and stir in garlic, salt and pepper. Cover slices with puree and bake in hot over (400° F.) for 15 minutes or till tops begin to brown. Serve at once.

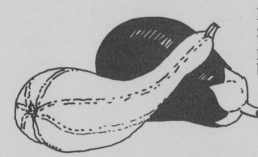

Braised Celery

This recipe has long been a classic in France — but its simplicity strikes many Americans as a delightful novelty.

> *1 bunch fresh white celery*
> *1 cup white stock*
> *2 tablespoons melted butter*
> *OR — 1 cup HOLLANDAISE SAUCE (see recipe)*

Wash celery one branch at a time and cut away leaf ends and stem core. Chop branches into 3-inch sections. Heat stock till just at boiling point in Calphalon sauteuse or omelet pan. Add celery and simmer till barely tender. Top with melted butter or *HOLLANDAISE SAUCE* and serve at once.

Sauteed Romaine

For many people romaine tends to be a bit tough as a salad green —
but the following recipe suggests a finer destiny for this handsome
vegetable.

1 head romaine
1 slice onion
1 clove
1 teaspoon salt
1 teaspoon white vinegar
2 tablespoons melted butter
1/2 cup water

Rinse romaine head and shake out as much water as possible. Slice
crosswise in 1-inch slices. Pour butter, water, and vinegar into
Calphalon sauteuse and bring to boiling point. Add onion, clove, and
salt and simmer uncovered till liquid is almost gone. Toss romaine in
boiled-down liquid, cover pan, and simmer at lowest heat possible,
stirring occasionally. When leaf ends are tender serve at once.
(Remove clove if you see it.)

Broccoli Valhalla

1 large or 2 small heads fresh broccoli
1 cup white stock or reconstituted chicken
   bouillon crystals
Yolks of 2 hard-boiled eggs

Wash broccoli and blot dry. Cut away tough part of stalks, leaving only flowers and slender branch-ends. In Calphalon sauteuse, bring stock to boil and add broccoli. Simmer covered till stems are just tender. Drain and serve, garnished with crumbled egg yolks.

Parsleyed Cauliflower

1 head very fresh cauliflower
4 cups water
1 teaspoon salt
3 tablespoons melted butter
1/4 cup fresh grated parsley

Wash cauliflower and blot dry. Cut away tough part of stems. Bring salted water to boil in bottom of Calphalon steamer, then fill upper part with cauliflower, cover, and reduce heat. Steam till tender — about 10 to 15 minutes. Just before serving, pour melted butter over cauliflower and sprinkle with grated parsley.

Tomates Farcies
(Broiled Stuffed Tomatoes)

Almost anything makes a good stuffing with this recipe — including ground leftover meats. Consider the following formula a savory take-off point, to which you may want to add other ingredients next time you make it.

6 medium tomatoes, or one per person
1 cup stale bread crumbs
1/4 cup each: chopped onion, mushrooms,
*   grated gruyere cheese, and parsley*
2 tablespoons Maggi seasoning
3 tablespoons peanut oil

Wash and dry tomatoes. Remove cores and chop fine. Heat oil in Calphalon butter warmer and add onion and mushrooms. Toss till lightly browned. Add crumbs and continue tossing till thoroughly blended. Turn off heat and toss in cheese, parsley, Maggi seasoning, and chopped tomatoes. Arrange cored tomatoes on baking sheet and stuff till heaping with crumb mixture. Set oven to broil, but bake tomatoes on lowest shelf for 8 minutes. Then pass them under broiler to brown, 3 to 5 minutes. Lift them from pan with slotted spoon and serve at once.

Austrian Cabbage

1 small green head of cabbage
3 tablespoons peanut oil
1 tablespoon Maggi seasoning
1/2 teaspoon each: salt, paprika, powdered onion
1 cup concentrated milk

Chop cabbage fine and saute it in oil, using Calphalon omelet pan or sauteuse. Add seasonings and toss with fork to blend thoroughly. Pour milk over all and bake in medium oven (350° F.) for about 30 minutes.

Corn Saute

Here is an interesting way to use leftover corn-on-the-cob — but of course it's better fresh.

Slice corn from cob — one for each person if possible
2 tablespoons peanut oil
1/2 cup finely chopped onion
1/2 cup chopped pimiento-stuffed olives
salt and pepper to taste

Heat oil in Calphalon omelet pan or sauteuse. Saute onion till golden. Add corn, and olives and saute 3 to 4 minutes longer. Add salt and pepper and serve sizzling.

Mushrooms Milano
(Mushrooms Stuffed with Fresh Spinach)

12 large fresh mushrooms (or 3 per person)
1 bunch fresh spinach
1 cup cottage cheese
1/3 cup grated parmesan cheese or sharp grated gruyere
1 tablespoon melted butter
1 tablespoon peanut oil
1 pinch each: garlic powder, ground black pepper

Wash and blot mushrooms dry. Cut away stems and mince fine. Mix butter and oil and brush caps thoroughly with this mixture. Arrange caps in Calphalon omelet pan. Wash spinach twice and drain. Remove stems and chop leaves fine. Stir in cottage cheese and seasonings, top with cheese. Bake in hot oven (450° F.) for 10 minutes.

NOTE: This recipe makes a handsome canape. Use medium-size mushrooms for about 3 dozen.

Bok Choy with Bacon Bits
(Chinese Chard Flavored with Bacon)

1 bunch fresh bok choy
2 strips lean bacon or 1 thin slice of smoked ham
4 cups water
1 teaspoon salt

Wash bok choy like spinach and drain or shake dry. Saute bacon slowly, till golden but not brown — just to the crumbling stage. Bring water and salt to boil in bottom of Calphalon steamer, then add cut up bok choy to top. Steam for 10 minutes or till stems are tender. Toss bok choy in serving dish with bacon drippings and crumbled or chopped bacon bits.

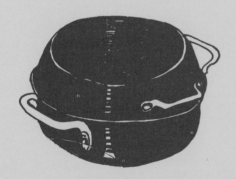

Herbed Cucumbers

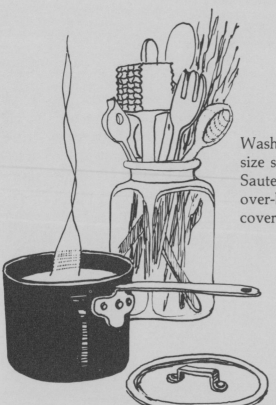

2 ripe medium cucumbers
1 small onion
2 tablespoons peanut oil
2 tablespoons chopped fresh mint
1 teaspoon salt
1 dash angostura bitters
2 tablespoons water

Wash and dry cucumbers. Slice thin, with skins. Slice onion in same size slices. In Calphalon omelet pan or sauteuse, heat oil with salt. Saute vegetables about 3 minutes, turning constantly to prevent over-browning. Add other ingredients, reduce heat, and simmer covered for 2 minutes more or till barely tender. Serve hot.

Cheese-Stuffed Baked Onions

6 medium-size onions or 1 per person
6 cherry tomatoes
1/2 cup grated sharp gruyere cheese
1/2 cup stale bread crumbs
1/4 cup fresh minced parsley
1/4 cup grated parmesan cheese
2 tablespoons peanut oil
1 teaspoon curry powder
1 tablespoon Maggi seasoning
NEW CUISINE WHITE SAUCE (see recipe)

Peel onions and cut off tough stem cap. Simmer in Calphalon sauteuse for half an hour or till just tender. Use salted water to cover bottom of pan up to 1/3 inch. (You may have to add water during cooking.) While onions are cooking, chop tomatoes and parsley, grate bread and cheeses. Toss these ingredients together, to make stuffing. Drain onions, reserving liquor, and remove centers. Fill onion shells with stuffing and arrange on baking sheet. Pour a little oil over each onion and bake at 400° F. for 30 minutes.

DURING BAKING — make NEW CUISINE WHITE SAUCE, substituting onion liquor for part of water. Stir curry powder, Maggi seasoning, and chopped onion centers into sauce and serve in sauceboat with baked hot onions.

Baked Onions Florentine

This savory dish is good either hot or cold and combines the technique for preparing CHEESE-STUFFED BAKED ONIONS (see preceding recipe) with the MUSHROOMS MILANO stuffing.

6 medium onions (or one per person)
Spinach-cheese stuffing (see recipe for
MUSHROOMS MILANO)

Cook onions till tender, drain and remove centers. (Save liquor and centers for soup.) Fill with spinach-cheese stuffing, omitting chopped mushroom stems unless you have them. (You can substitute a few chopped water chestnuts or 2 tablespoons minced celery.) Bake onions at 400° F. for about 30 minutes and serve hot. No sauce is necessary.

Ratatouille Nicoise

This recipe is delicious either hot or cold, and like any great medley it tastes better the second day. Perhaps this is lucky, because there's no such thing as a "small" ratatouille.

3 ripe zucchini squashes
1 small eggplant
4 medium tomatoes
1 large or 2 small onions
5 tablespoons peanut oil
1 cup pitted ripe olives
2 tablespoons salt
1 tablespoon coarse ground black pepper
1 pinch finely powdered dry oregano

Wash, peel, and cut up zucchini and eggplant in 1-inch pieces. Quarter tomatoes and onions. In Calphalon sauteuse warm oil. Add all other ingredients except olives and simmer till tender. Stir in olives and serve hot or cold.

Spinach Madeira

Traditionally enjoyed as a separate course in France, Spinach Madeira is the apotheosis of a humble garden vegetable. Thanks to the modern kitchen blender, its preparation has been vastly simplified, and I hope its originators will forgive me if I recommend it as a beautiful accessory to steak, chops, and boiled ham.

2 bunches fresh spinach
1 tablespoon unsalted butter
1/4 cup condensed or concentrated milk
1 cup sliced fresh mushrooms
1 cup croutons, sauteed
4 tablespoons madeira wine
1 dash each: nutmeg, salt, pepper

Wash spinach thoroughly and steam till just tender in Calphalon sauteuse — about 10 minutes. (Use smallest amount of water possible in bottom of steamer.) Put spinach through blender with milk, but do not puree. Stop blender and scrape sides every few seconds till spinach reaches "fine-chopped" stage. Saute mushrooms in butter, then add madeira a few drops at a time, cooking as quickly as possible to keep mushrooms light. Stir in spinach and seasonings, and reheat. Top with croutons browned in oil.

Summer Squash with Chives

2 pounds fresh summer squash
1/8 cup melted butter
1/8 cup peanut oil
1 teaspoon lemon juice
3 tablespoons chopped fresh chives
salt and pepper to taste

Wash dry, and cut up squash. Steam for 10 minutes in Calphalon steamer — or till tender. Melt butter, stir in oil and lemon juice. Turn squash into serving dish and pour butter mixture over all. Lightly salt and pepper squash, top with chives and serve.

Brussels Sprouts Hollandaise

1 pound small brussels sprouts
4 cups water
1 teaspoon salt
NEW CUISINE EASY HOLLANDAISE SAUCE
(see recipe)

Wash sprouts, cut away stem ends, and drain in top of Calphalon steamer. Bring water and salt to boil in bottom of steamer, add sprouts and reduce heat. Steam sprouts for 10 minutes or till just tender. Serve with Hollandaise Sauce.

Petit-Pois Medley

This pretty mixture of new garden vegetables makes proper use of tiny new peas, which are so sweet and aromatic they here serve as a flavoring.

2 large beefsteak tomatoes
4 cups white celery, chopped
1 cup fresh tiny peas or 1 package
  thawed tiny frozen peas
1 teaspoon salt
1/4 teaspoon sugar
1 leaf fresh thyme
1 pinch onion powder

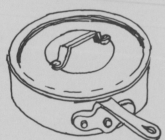

Heat oil in Calphalon sauteuse. Add celery, tomatoes, salt, sugar, thyme leaf and onion powder and simmer lightly, stirring occasionally till celery is tender — about 5 minutes. Add peas without stirring and simmer 5 minutes more, covered. Turn off heat (or remove pan if cooking electrically), and let pan stand in warm place for 10 minutes more. Toss vegetables once or twice with fork and serve.

Green Bean Souffle

The attraction of this dish is that the beans cook just to the point of crispness and the recipe calls for only one tablespoon of flour. Try it in winter with any roast and a second vegetable (instead of potatoes), or in summer with cold boiled ham.

1 pound fresh green beans	3 sprigs fresh parsley
OR — 1 10-ounce package frozen	1 whole clove
French-cut green beans	1 bay leaf
1 cup concentrated or condensed milk	1 tablespoon flour
1 tablespoon chopped onion	1/2 teaspoon salt
4 tablespoons peanut oil	3 eggs

Remove ends and strings from beans, and cut julienne style in thin lengthwise strips. (If using frozen beans, thaw, drain, and blot dry. Reduce milk by 1 tablespoon.) In Calphalon butter warmer, heat milk with bay leaf, clove and parsley. Turn off or remove from heat when milk shows first sign of foaming at the edge of pan. In medium-size Calphalon omelet pan or sauteuse, heat oil and cook onion till tender but not browned. Blend in flour and salt. Pour seasoned milk through strainer into flour mixture and cook stirring constantly till mixture thickens and comes to boil. Remove from heat. Separate eggs and beat whites till stiff. Stir yolks, then beans into sauce; fold in egg whites. Sprinkle top with grated nutmeg, dash of curry powder, or paprika. Bake in medium oven (350° F.) for 20 to 25 minutes and serve at once.

Lechuga Rellena
(Cheese-Stuffed Lettuce with Tomato)

This delightful dish might have been developed during the brief time Napoleon II's army was stationed in Mexico. In style it resembles the much spicier *chili relleno* — yet it owes much to French cooks too, who have long regarded lettuce as an interesting vegetable for the cooking pot.

8 large green outer lettuce leaves (or 2 per person)
1/2 lb. mild gruyere, jack, or white cheddar cheese
4 medium tomatoes
1 small onion
1 teaspoon salt
1 dash each: garlic powder, cayenne pepper
4 tablespoons peanut oil
2 eggs
3 tablespoons enriched white flour
1 dash seasoning salt

Wash and steam lettuce in Calphalon steamer till no longer crisp — about 3 minutes. Divide cheese into 8 pieces and roll each one in a lettuce leaf. Beat egg yolks and whites separately: yolks should be foamy, whites stiff. Beat flour and seasoning salt into yolks, then fold in egg whites, to make a fairly stiff batter. Warm half of oil in Calphalon sauteuse. Dip lettuce rolls in batter, arrange in sauteuse to simmer gently. When cooked, batter should puff up and look dry on top. Turn carefully, and serve topped with *Tomato-Onion Sauce.*

TO MAKE SAUCE:

Simmer chopped tomatoes and onions in remaining half of oil with seasonings. When tomatoes are tender, spoon sauce over lettuce rolls and serve at once.

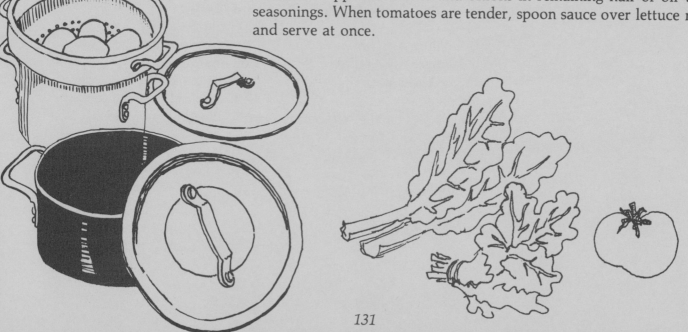

Oriental Zucchini

1 pound fresh zucchini (about 3 medium)
1 cup chopped onions
2 tablespoons peanut oil
1 small piece fresh ginger, crushed
OR — 1/8 teaspoon ground ginger
1/4 cup sherry (medium sweet)
1/8 cup soy sauce
2 teaspoons sesame seeds, toasted

In medium Calphalon omelet pan or sauteuse, heat oil. Add onions and ginger and stir over heat till onions are cooked to translucent stage. Add sherry a few drops at a time to scald out alcohol. Add peeled cut-up zucchini and toss with fork till cooked tender. Add Maggi, soy sauce, and sesame seeds, blending throroughly. Salt if necessary and serve.

Vegetables Vinaigrette

This dish is meant to look a trifle unrefined, so don't cut up vegetables too fine. An ideal mixture would be whole small Belgian carrots, sugar peas in the pods, whole green beans, and coarse-chopped celery. You may also use fresh asparagus, eggplant, various squashes, or whatever is in season.

About 4 cups fresh vegetables (or 1 cup per person)
1 cup peanut oil
5 tablespoons white wine vinegar
OR — 5 tablespoons fresh lemon juice
   1 teaspoon salt
   1/4 teaspoon fresh ground black pepper
   1 pinch tarragon (dried)
OR — 1 leaf fresh tarragon, cut up
1 tablespoon grated fresh parsley

Wash vegetables and cook in Calphalon steamer for 10 minutes. Blend all other ingredients thoroughly. Arrange vegetables in serving dish and pour marinade over all. Chill overnight in refrigerator. Serve cold as summer vegetable, or as winter hors-d'oeuvre or salad course.

Mongolian Asparagus

Granted that nothing surpasses the exquisite simplicity of fresh steamed asparagus with melted butter. The following recipe, however, is a delightful alternative for those who want to make the most of the short asparagus season.

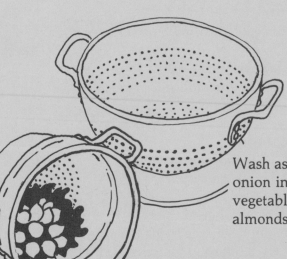

1½ pounds fresh asparagus
1 small onion
1 teaspoon chicken bouillon crystals
1/4 cup peanut oil
1/4 cup sliced blanched almonds
Juice of 1/2 lemon
1/2 teaspoon grated lemon peel

Wash asparagus and cut tender part of stalks into 1-inch pieces. Cut onion into thin slices. Heat oil in Calphalon omelet pan and stir-fry vegetables with bouillon crystals till tender but not brown. Stir in almonds, lemon juice, and peel, and serve hot.

Bavarian Red Cabbage

Red cabbage is often overlooked as a menu possibility, though it has much to commend it. Rich in Vitamin C, often cheaper than potatoes, red cabbage keeps well, cooks quickly, and brightens both salads and dinner plates.

1 small to medium head red cabbage
1/2 cup salted water
1 tablespoon wine vinegar
1 tablespoon sugar
(OPTIONAL — 1 tablespoon carraway seeds)

Wash cabbage and slice crosswise into fine shreds, cutting around core. (You may save core to shred into an elegant salad or cook in a soup.) In a medium size Calphalon sauteuse, heat salted water, vinegar, sugar, and carraway if you're using it. When water comes to boil, add cabbage and cook covered at low heat for about 10 minutes. Stir occasionally to make sure cabbage is not cooking too fast, and add a tablespoon of water if necessary. Serve with hot roast pork, chicken, or veal.

Salads

CHAPTER TEN

SALADS

Growing up in the Midwest, I used to think we had the salad course worked out perfectly. It was served on a side plate, along with the main course, and you could intersperse a cool crisp bit of it between forkfuls of hot and heartier foods. Later I fell in love with the French custom of serving salads between the main course and dessert; and now as a Californian I find I have to demur to the busboy to prevent him from whisking away my half-eaten salad to make way for the entree.

One delight of dining at home is that you can arrange such things exactly as you please. If your table is crowded, it might make sense to serve the salad separately, either before or after the meat. But if you want to cut down on dishwashing, you can deal with your salad Midwestern style, serving it on the bread plate alongside the main course, or even on the same plate.

Some of the following recipes can be served without lettuce. But none of them includes the whipped-cream-and-marshmallow concoctions that used to call themselves salads under the "old cuisine."

Spinach Salad with Lemon-Yogurt Dressing

1 bunch fresh spinach
1/2 cup Yogurt (see recipe)
Juice from 1 lemon
1 teaspoon grated lemon peel
salt
fresh ground pepper

Wash spinach twice and blot dry. Remove stems and tear leaves into pieces that can be easily managed with a fork. Mix yogurt and lemon juice, then add enough salt to cut acidity of the dressing — about 1 teaspoonful. Just before serving, toss salad with dressing, and grate pepper over all.

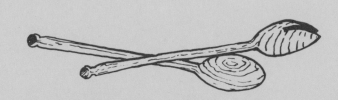

Celeriac Marine

Among aficionados, the root of the celery is a delicacy that far surpasses its less expensive cousin the stalk. One small or medium root can serve 4 to 8 people generously.

1 celery root
1 cup peanut oil
5 tablespoons red wine vinegar
1 slice onion
1 teaspoon salt
fresh ground black pepper

Peel root and cut away tips and stem end, till you end up with a perfect whitish nugget. Slice root crosswise in thin, quarter-inch slices. If the root is very large, you may want to halve it vertically before slicing. Mix oil, vinegar, onion and salt. Place celery slices in bowl and cover with marinade. Refrigerate covered for 12 hours or overnight. To serve, arrange slices on a leaf of bib or limestone lettuce. Remove onion and spoon marinade over celery root. Garnish with very light sprinkling of fresh ground pepper.

NOTE: To serve the same day, you can shorten marinating time by steaming root for 5 minutes before slicing.

Salade de Champignons
(Mushroom Salad)

1/2 pound fresh white mushrooms
1 cup peanut oil
3 tablespoons red wine vinegar
2 tablespoons fresh lemon juice
1 pinch salt
1 teaspoon fresh chopped chives
1 teaspoon fresh grated parsley

Wash and dry mushrooms but do not peel. Slice thinly in vertical slices including stems. Mix oil, vinegar, lemon juice, and salt. Pour marinade ove mushrooms and toss lightly to blend. Let mushrooms absorb dressing for about an hour. Serve on lettuce leaf and top with chives and parsley.

Salad Kee Joon

The following recipe is called "Sai See Gai" at the famous KEE JOON'S penthouse restaurant overlooking San Francisco Bay. It makes rather large helpings for four, but I've never run across anyone who couldn't finish it!

1/2 of roasting chicken (over 3 pounds whole)
1/2 cup crushed toasted almonds
2 teaspoons toasted sesame seeds
1/2 cup sweet red ginger preserve*
1/2 bunch Cinese parsley
1/2 head lettuce
6 green onions
Tapioca flour — about 1 cup*
Wanton skins — 1 dozen*

SAUCE:
2 tablespoons plum sauce*
2 tablespoons Chinese apricot sauce*
1 tablespoon light soy sauce
1 tablespoon sesame oil
1 teaspoon powdered hot mustard (liquify with 4 teaspoons water)

Steam chicken in Calphalon steamer for about 25 minutes. During cooking, prepare a pan of tapioca flour. When chicken is cooked, cover skin completely with flour. Then steam again for 15 to 25 minutes. Then refrigerate, at least one hour. When chicken is cold, heat oil in bottom of Calphalon deep fryer and fry chicken to a golden brown — about 10 or 15 minutes. When cool enough to handle, bone meat and cut into thin strips — about 1½-inches — including skin.

Mix ingredients for sauce and pour over chicken, tossing to blend thoroughly. Sprinkle almonds and sesame seeds over chicken and toss again. Mix in finely shredded lettuce, ginger preserve, parsley leaves, and white part of onions chopped fine. Serve at once, with deep-fried wanton skins.

NOTE: Unused chicken half may be frozen in one piece or in strips, to be used later in galantine, chicken salad, pate or Shepherd's Pie.

* Available in Chinese grocery store if not in regular market.

Leaf Lettuce Pimiento

There is, of course, no end to the possible combinations you can come up with by uniting fresh vegetables, dressing, and garnish. The following recipe might just as easily work with Belgian endive, or artichoke hearts, instead of lettuce; and you could substitute capers or grated hard-cooked egg yolk for pimientos. In fact, I hope you will some time. But this recipe is a classic for its simplicity and beauty.

1 head leaf lettuce — limestone, bib,
*   or any of the tender varieties*
4 tablespoons peanut oil
1 tablespoon red wine vinegar
1 pinch salt
1/4 cup chopped pimiento strips

Wash and dry lettuce thoroughly. Tear up large leaves but not the smaller ones, and place in a salad bowl — ideally a transparent one. Pour oil over leaves and toss till leaves are thoroughly coated. Sprinkle vinegar on lettuce and toss again till flavor is blended through. Add salt, gradually, and toss once more. Sprinkle pimientos over salad and serve as soon as possible.

Desserts

C. Schneider

CHAPTER ELEVEN

DESSERTS

New Cuisine desserts are the kind that never give anyone a guilt complex. They are just that "little something sweet" that performs like the dot at the end of a poem: small, perfect, and final.

Apricot Alaska

1 pound fresh apricots
1 ounce unflavored gelatin crystals
1 tablespoon fresh lemon juice
1/2 cup boiling water
2 eggs, separated
1 teaspoon grated nutmeg

Wash and pit apricots, then puree in blender. Soften gelatin in lemon juice, then stir into boiling water. Add gelatin, nutmeg and egg yolks to blender and mix thoroughly — about 30 seconds on low speed. Pour mixture into ovenproof bowl and chill till set. Beat egg whites till stiff and add a pinch of salt, sugar, or cream of tartar to maintain consistency. When apricots are firm, unmold and cover with egg whites. Pass under broiler to brown egg whites (about 2 minutes) and serve at once.

Home-Made Yogurt

In its purest form, yogurt is a kitchen staple I couldn't do without. Its performance in salad dressings, casseroles, stroganoff or soup lends that indefinable something that both baffles and intrigues the palate. As a dessert, plain yogurt is admittedly an acquired taste. But flavored with honey, fresh fruits, brown sugar and cinnamon, creme de cacao or creme de menthe, glacéed fruits, concentrated orange juice, rum-soaked raisins, home-made jams or jellies, and probably many flavors that I have yet to discover — yogurt makes a hearty, nutritious, and profoundly satisfying dessert.

The following method makes 2 quarts of yogurt, which can be stored almost indefinitely in your refrigerator. When the supply gets down to one cup, use the remainder as a culture for a new batch.

1 8-ounce carton plain yogurt (culture)
4 cups water, lukewarm
3 cups nonfat dry milk
3 cups concentrated milk

Fill blender with half of water and liquify dry milk. Pour mixture into 9-inch Calphalon sauteuse. Add remaining water and concentrated milk, and stir. Heat slowly till mixture begins to steam. Remove pan from heat and cool in a basin of cold water. While mixture cools, stir yogurt in carton to soften, then pour it into bottom of any two-quart container, plastic or glass, which you can seal with a fitted cover. When milk mixture reaches room temperature, stir it into yogurt a little at a time till thoroughly blended. Cover container and set in the bottom of your Calphalon steamer, filled with enough warm water to reach just to the level of the yogurt mixture inside the inner container. Cover the steamer and put in a warm place for at least 4 hours, but perhaps overnight. When mixture reaches a thick custardy stage — like half-set gelatin — take inner container out of water bath and refrigerate till solid.

Kadota Figs in Red Wine

Many people find the sweetness of fresh kadota figs almost overpowering. The following recipe was developed by a chef who describes it as "a celebration of cruel contrasts." Cruel it isn't, but a celebration it is indeed.

1 pound fresh kadota figs
OR — 1 can of figs, well drained
1 cup red Burgundy wine
2 tablespoons unsalted butter
2 tablespoons chopped blanched almonds
OR — 2 tablespoons unsweetened coconut

Wash figs and place them in shallow-bottomed bowl or Calphalon butter warmer. Pour wine over figs and marinate all day or overnight. Spoon wine over figs from time to time if not fully covered. Just before serving, drain figs and place them in dessert dishes or sherbet goblets. Pour marinade into pitcher or measuring beaker Heat butter to sizzling stage in Calphalon butter warmer, and add wine marinade a few drops at a time till it becomes a rich caramelized glaze. Pour a little over each dish of figs and serve with almonds or coconut garnish.

Merengues Tenchita
(Hortensia's Meringues)

Meringues of all types epitomize the New Cuisine-style dessert. They're light, airy, made with the simplest ingredients, and combine with fresh fruits in a blaze of glory. The following recipe, from Peru, goes well with after-dinner coffee, but it also brightens lunch sacks, tea trays, and everything in between.

> 6 egg whites
> 2 cups powdered sugar, sifted twice after measuring
> 1/4 teaspoon cream of tartar
> a few caramels, cut into small bits

Beat egg whites till they stand stiff, "in snowy points." Add sugar and cream of tartar gradually. When thoroughly combined, drop mixture by large spoonfuls on a very lightly oiled baking sheet. Decorate tops with caramel bits. Bake at 275° F. for 40 minutes. Then turn oven off and leave meringues inside till cool.

Pavlova
(Australian Meringue with Fruit)

This dessert is the Aussie counterpart to Yankee shortcake, and it's served in roughly the same manner. As you will see, however, there's no comparison in taste or texture.

6 egg whites
12 ounces (or 12 tablespoons) granulated white sugar
1 teaspoon vinegar
1/2 pint whipped cream*
A mixture of fresh fruit — strawberries, bananas, peaches, blueberries — whatever's in season

Beat egg whites till fluffy, add sugar gradually, and vinegar last of all. Shape a square of aluminum foil into a shallow, round or square baking "pan" and oil it lightly. Spread mixture evenly into "pan" and bake 1½ hours at 250° F. When *Pavlova* is cool and ready to serve, peel away foil. Heap it with fruit and top with whipped cream.

* OR — See recipe for DELGADO DESSERT TOPPING

Orange Blossom Meringues

1 cup dried apricots
1/4 cup (approximately) fresh orange juice
5 egg whites
1 teaspoon vanilla extract
2 cups granulated white sugar
1/4 teaspoon cream of tartar
1 cup walnuts, chopped fine

Soak apricots in orange juice for one hour or till barely soft. Drain apricots dry* and chop fine. Beat egg whites till stiff, with cream of tartar, then add in sugar slowly. When mixture is thick and glossy, stir in walnuts and apricots. Spoon meringues onto baking sheets lined with brown paper (prepare enough for about 7 dozen). Bake on highest shelf of oven at 225° F. for 25 to 30 minutes.

* Leftover juice can be used to make DELGADO DESSERT TOPPING (see recipe).

Fresh Apple Cake

2½ cups peeled, chopped apple
1 cup sugar
1/2 cup melted butter
1 egg
1½ cups flour
1 teaspoon baking soda
1 teaspoon salt
1/2 cup raisins
1/2 cup chopped walnuts
3/4 teaspoons cinnamon

Stir sugar into apples and let stand, about 5 minutes. Blend butter and egg into apple mix. Then stir in flour, baking soda and salt, tossing to mix thoroughly. Add raisins, walnuts and cinnamon, and blend. Bake cake in greased, floured 8 x 8-inch pan, at 350° F. for 50 minutes. Cool at least 10 minutes before removing from pan. Serve topped with *VANILLA SUGAR* (see recipe) or *DELGADO DESSERT TOPPING* (see recipe).

Pineapple with White Wine

> 1 whole fresh pineapple
> 2 cups (approximately) light wine — any of the
>   German wines or a good California Rhine type
> 1 cup VANILLA SUGAR (see recipe)
> OR — 1 cup coarsely shredded coconut

Peel pineapple and cut out core — but do not cut all the way through center. Your pineapple must function like a bowl — into which you pour the wine, as much as it will hold. Chill the whole thing for 24 hours. Serve by slicing pineapple crosswise, in rings, with plenty of juice. Garnish with *VANILLA SUGAR* or coconut.

VANILLA SUGAR

> 1 vanilla bean (dried)
> 1 pound confectioner's sugar

Place sugar in canister or storage container with tightly fitting cover. Break vanilla bean into two or three pieces and add to cannister. Cover and shake. Store sugar for at least a week before using.

Cheese Cake Sylphide

2 packets (2 ounces) unflavored gelatin
3/4 cup sugar
1/4 teaspoon salt
2 eggs
1 cup skim or reconstituted nonfat
    dry milk
1 teaspoon grated lemon rind
1/3 cup graham cracker crumbs
1/8 teaspoon cinnamon
1/8 teaspoon nutmeg
3 cups large curd cottage cheese
    (1½ pints)
1 teaspoon vanilla extract
DELGADO DESSERT TOPPING

The texture of this elegant cake is smooth and creamy, but lighter than most cheese cakes. Needless to say, it gets its name from this airy quality — but I like to think it also means you can enjoy it without affecting your sylph-like silhouette.

Mix gelatin, 1/2 cup of sugar, and salt together in Calphalon saucepan, or top of double boiler. Separate eggs. Beat yolks together with milk and add to gelatin mixture. Over very low heat (or boiling water), stir constantly till gelatin is thoroughly dissolved — about 5 minutes. Remove from heat, and stir in lemon rind. Refrigerate pan till mixture thickens slightly, like custard. Meanwhile combine crumbs, cinnamon, and nutmeg and set aside. Puree cottage cheese in blender with vanilla, and stir into chilled gelatin mixture. Whip egg whites till very stiff and gradually beat in remaining sugar. Fold into gelatin mixture. Prepare one recipe *DELGADO DESSERT TOPPING** (makes about 2-2½ cups), and fold this last of all into mixture. Smooth mixture into 8-inch spring-form pan and top with crumbs. Refrigerate for at least 4 hours before serving.

* Omitting sugar.

Delgado Dessert Topping

This recipe can be used wherever you might use a whipped cream topping. However, it lacks the "durability" of fat-based toppings, so it should be served at once. It can be used in any dessert recipe that also calls for egg yolks or gelatin (*CHEESE CAKE SYLPHIDE*, for example), but not in a recipe that gets its stability only from beaten egg whites. It can be used in making ice-box cakes, but will result in a rather firm and unlayered "trifle," which goes well topped with fresh fruit, rum-soaked raisins, or any other dessert topping.

1½ cups nonfat dry milk
1/3 cup icewater
1/4 cup sugar
1 teaspoon vanilla
1 tablespoon fresh lemon juice
OR 1 tablespoon frozen orange concentrate

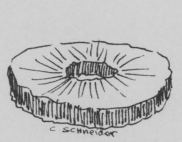

EPILOG

If you cook the way I do, you know that these recipes — no matter how enthusiastically I've described them — can always be improved, amended, and tampered with in a million creative ways. Cooking (and eating, too) is an art form. The dishes you turn out in your kitchen-studio may never look, taste, smell, and caress the palate exactly the same way twice in a row — depending as they do on the temperature of every tool you use and the infinite whims of Mother Nature. In fairness I should add that not everyone can taste the tiny differences I'm describing — and those who can are likely to enjoy the subtle variety.

On the other hand, if you set out with the firm intention of changing and improving any of these recipes, do it with my blessings. For one artist to inspire another is the greatest achievement of all.

BIBLIOGRAPHY

The author wishes to commend the following authors, publications, and individuals who helped to inspire this book:

Chamberlain, Narcissa and Narcisse, *The Chamberlain Calendar of French Cooking*. New York: Hastings House, 1968.
Crigson, Jane, ed. *The World Atlas of Food*. London: Mitchell Beazley Publishers, Ltd. 1974.
MacMiadhachain, Anna, *Spanish Regional Cookery*. Harmondsworth, Middlesex, England: Penguin Books Ltd., 1976.
H. J. Heinz Company, *Facts about Foods*. Pittsburgh: 1960.
Norman, Barbara, *The Spanish Cookbook*. New York: Bantam Books, Inc. 1975.
Pappas, Lou Seibert, *Greek Cooking*. New York: Harper and Row, Publishers, 1973.
Rombauer, Irma S. and Becker, Marion Rombauer, *The Joy of Cooking*. Indianapolis: Bobbs-Merrill Company, Inc., 1953.
Simon, Andre, *Andre Simon's French Cook Book*. New York: Crosset and Dunlap, Publishers, 1948.
Wolfe, Kenneth C. *Cooking for the Professional Chef: A Structured Approach*. Albany, New York: Delmar Publishers, 1976.
Nancy Baker
Carlos Maximo Benavides
Sra. Hortensia Benavides de Fauche
Kathleen Bigbee
Jorge Brughera
Janice Brumbaum
Sra. Celia Cordero
Rosa Fauche de Carrillo
Edith Race Goodale
Alan Maruice Campbell Holmes
Jenny van Isendyck Holmes
Joanna E. Holmes
Marie Jeffrey
Kee Joon's Cuisine of China Penthouse Restaurant, Burlingame, California
Mary J. Kinney
Jean H. Lamb
Sandra T. Lehman
Sra. Irene Niguez de Juliussen
Mme. Francoise Ollivier
Katherine S. Pelan
Nancy Pourciau
Vicki Hale Riley
Dorothy James Roberts
Aileene Mattes Roth
Eugenio Sos Roy, Conde de Gondomar National Parador, Bayona, Spain
Jerome Steimle
Nancy Howrie Thompson
Patricia Burroughs Vadopalas

Index